Collateralized
Loan
Obligations

MASTERING CLO INVESTING

Collateralized Loan Obligations Structure

by

John King

Expert in Loan Obligations

Copyright Page

INTRODUCTION

Collateralized Loan Obligations (CLOs) are a rapidly growing segment of the fixed-income market, with the global CLO market reaching over **$700 billion** in outstanding assets as of 2023. CLOs are structured products that pool together corporate loans, primarily leveraged loans, and divide them into tranches with varying risk and return profiles. The CLO market has seen impressive growth in recent years, with new issuance exceeding **$130 billion** in 2022 alone, despite global economic uncertainties.

These products are attractive to investors seeking higher yields compared to traditional investment-grade securities, with CLO equity tranches offering annual returns in the range of **8-15%**, depending on the risk profile and market conditions. CLOs are actively managed, meaning that a portfolio manager oversees the loans within the CLO, aiming to optimize returns by buying and selling loans as market conditions change.

The structure of CLOs, with senior, mezzanine, and equity tranches, allows for a broad range of risk exposures, from the safer senior tranches (rated **AAA** or **AA**) to the higher-risk equity tranches. This diversification, combined with the potential for attractive yields, has made CLO investing increasingly popular among institutional investors, hedge funds, and even individual investors through funds and ETFs.

Despite their appeal, CLOs come with inherent risks, including **credit risk**, **interest rate risk**, and **liquidity risk**, which investors must carefully evaluate. However, for those willing to navigate the complexities of CLO investing, the potential for strong returns remains a compelling factor, especially in a low-interest-rate environment.

Understanding Collateralized Loan Obligations (CLOs)

Collateralized Loan Obligations (CLOs) are complex investment vehicles backed by a pool of loans made to corporations. They have gained significant popularity in recent years as a way for investors to gain exposure to a diversified pool of loans, which can generate attractive returns. CLOs are often structured in a way that offers varying levels of risk and return, providing options for a wide range of investors, from institutional investors to high-net-worth individuals.

How CLOs Work

A CLO is created by pooling together loans from various corporate borrowers, typically non-investment grade companies, and then dividing this pool into different tranches or layers. These tranches represent different levels of risk and reward, and each tranche is sold to investors in the CLO market. The manager of the CLO, known as the CLO manager, actively buys and sells loans within the pool in an effort to enhance returns and minimize risks.

Most of the debt in a CLO is secured by high-quality collateral, which adds an additional layer of protection for investors. CLOs are designed to withstand market volatility by providing a diversified portfolio of loans, with a built-in hierarchy of tranches that ensures senior investors are paid first in case of liquidation.

Types of CLO Tranches

CLOs consist of two main types of tranches: debt tranches and equity tranches. Debt tranches, sometimes referred to as mezzanine tranches, are treated similarly to bonds, as they offer a specified stream of interest payments and principal repayment. These tranches are ranked in terms of seniority, with the highest-rated tranches having the lowest risk and lowest returns, while the lower-rated tranches offer higher yields at a higher level of risk.

Equity tranches, on the other hand, are paid last and do not provide regular cash flows. These tranches offer ownership in the CLO itself, giving investors the potential for higher returns if the CLO is successfully sold or refinanced. While equity tranche investors face significant risk, they have the opportunity to earn substantial returns, as the excess cash flow from the CLO after all debt obligations are met is paid to them.

CLO Structure and Hierarchy

The structure of a CLO is designed to provide a layered approach to risk and reward. The debt tranches are typically divided into the following categories:

- **AAA Tranche**: The highest-rated tranche, offering the lowest risk and lowest return.
- **AA Tranche**: Slightly higher risk than the AAA tranche, with a correspondingly higher return.
- **A Tranche**: A moderate-risk tranche with a reasonable return.
- **BBB Tranche**: A lower-rated tranche that offers higher returns but comes with more risk.
- **BB Tranche**: A highly speculative tranche with significantly higher returns but higher risk.
- **Equity Tranche**: The lowest-ranked tranche, which provides the highest potential return, but with the highest risk.

As a CLO enters the repayment phase, the higher-ranked tranches are paid first, followed by the lower-ranked tranches. Investors in the equity tranche are typically the last to be paid, but they can also reap the rewards if the CLO performs well.

The CLO Creation Process

The creation of a CLO involves several key steps:

1. **Establish the Capital Structure**: The first step in creating

a CLO is determining the capital structure, which involves setting the different levels of debt and equity that will back the CLO securities.

2. **Raise Capital**: Investors are then invited to contribute capital in exchange for various CLO tranches. The capital raised is used to buy loans from corporate borrowers.
3. **Select Tranches**: Investors choose which tranche they would like to invest in based on their risk tolerance and desired return profile.
4. **Purchase Loans**: The CLO manager uses the raised capital to buy a portfolio of loans from different borrowers, typically focusing on loans made to non-investment grade companies.
5. **Create a Special Purpose Vehicle (SPV)**: A special purpose vehicle is often established to issue CLO securities, providing additional protection to investors in the event of a default.
6. **Distribute Payments to Investors**: Once the CLO is up and running, the proceeds from the underlying loans are used to pay investors, with higher-ranked tranches being paid first.
7. **CLO Termination**: The CLO may be terminated once all securities have been repaid, or when the underlying loans have been paid off or sold.

Benefits of Investing in CLOs

Investing in CLOs can offer several benefits:

- **Portfolio Diversification**: CLOs allow investors to diversify their portfolios by gaining exposure to a pool of loans from various borrowers, which can reduce the risk of default from any single loan.

- **Higher Yields**: CLOs typically offer higher yields compared to other fixed-income investments such as government bonds or investment-grade corporate bonds, due to the higher risk associated with the underlying loans.
- **Credit Enhancement**: The structure of CLOs, with their different tranches, provides credit enhancement for senior tranche investors, giving them additional protection against losses from loan defaults.
- **Liquidity**: CLO securities are gencrally more liquid than the underlying loans, making them easier to buy and sell in the secondary market.
- **Professional Management**: CLOs are managed by experienced professionals who actively monitor the loan pool and adjust it as needed to improve performance.

Risks of Investing in CLOs

Despite the potential benefits, CLOs also come with risks:

- **Credit Risk**: CLOs are exposed to credit risk because the loans backing the CLOs are often made to non-investment grade borrowers. A rise in borrower defaults could lead to significant losses for investors, particularly those holding lower-ranked tranches.
- **Liquidity Risk**: CLO securities, while generally more liquid than the underlying loans, can still face liquidity risk, particularly during periods of market stress when it may be difficult to sell CLO securities.
- **Interest Rate Risk**: CLOs are subject to interest rate risk. If interest rates rise, the value of CLO securities could decrease, as their fixed interest rates become less attractive relative to new debt offerings.
- **Complexity**: CLOs are sophisticated investment vehicles,

and their structure can be difficult to understand. The complexity of CLOs may make it challenging for some investors to fully grasp the risks involved.

Who Buys CLOs?

CLOs are typically purchased by institutional investors, such as insurance companies, pension funds, and hedge funds. These investors are often looking for higher yields and are willing to take on additional risk in exchange for the potential for greater returns. Mutual funds, exchange-traded funds (ETFs), and collateralized fund obligations (CFOs) may also invest in CLOs, particularly in the junior tranches, which offer higher yields at higher risk.

Making Money with CLOs

Investing in CLOs can offer significant returns, especially for those who understand the risks involved. Investors can make money in CLOs by purchasing the higher-yielding, riskier tranches or by holding senior tranches for steady income. The key to success with CLOs is understanding the structure of the tranches and managing risk through diversification. With the right strategy, CLOs can be an attractive addition to an investment portfolio, offering both higher yields and diversified exposure to corporate debt.

Collateralized Loan Obligations (CLOs) are an attractive option for investors seeking higher yields and diversified exposure to non-investment grade corporate loans. While they come with inherent risks, including credit and liquidity risk, their structured approach and potential for high returns make them an appealing investment. Whether you're an institutional investor looking for secure senior debt or an investor seeking higher yields through equity tranches, CLOs offer a flexible and lucrative investment opportunity.

CHAPTER 1: THE FUNDAMENTALS OF CLO INVESTING

Section 1: What Are CLOs? Breaking Down the Basics

Collateralized Loan Obligations, commonly referred to as CLOs, are one of the most important and innovative financial instruments in the credit market. Simply put, a CLO is a type of structured finance product that pools together a collection of loans—typically corporate loans made to medium- to large-sized businesses—and packages them into a single investment vehicle. These loans, known as "leveraged loans," are generally issued to companies with below-investment-grade credit ratings, making them riskier but also higher-yielding than traditional corporate bonds.

Once these loans are bundled together, the CLO creates a structure that divides the cash flow generated by the loan pool into different layers, or "tranches." Each tranche represents a different level of risk and return. This unique structure allows investors to choose the level of risk and return that aligns with their investment preferences, ranging from highly secure, low-yield senior tranches to higher-risk, high-yield equity tranches.

CLOs play a critical role in modern financial markets by helping banks and financial institutions offload their corporate loans, thereby freeing up capital to make more loans. This, in turn, supports businesses by providing them with access to credit. For investors, CLOs offer a way to gain exposure to diversified portfolios of loans while benefiting from higher yields than traditional fixed-income instruments.

But why should CLOs matter to you as an investor? The answer lies in their resilience and performance history. CLOs have consistently outperformed other fixed-income investments in terms of returns, and their unique structure provides a natural cushion against loan defaults. Understanding CLOs, however, requires a clear grasp of their components, mechanisms, and role in the broader financial ecosystem.

Section 2: Key Components of a CLO

CLOs are composed of several interdependent components, all of which contribute to their function and appeal as an investment vehicle. To understand the fundamentals of CLO investing, it is crucial to break down these components:

1. **The Loan Pool**:
   At the heart of every CLO lies the pool of leveraged loans that serves as collateral. These loans are typically extended to companies with credit ratings below investment grade (e.g., BB+ or lower). Although these companies carry higher credit risk, they pay higher interest rates on their loans, which translates into higher potential returns for CLO investors.

   The loan pool is actively managed by a CLO manager, who is responsible for selecting, monitoring, and replacing loans to ensure the portfolio's performance aligns with the CLO's objectives. This active management sets CLOs apart from static pools of assets like mortgage-backed securities (MBS).

2. **The Tranche Structure**:
   CLOs are divided into several tranches, each representing a different level of risk and return. The typical structure includes:

   - **Senior Tranches**: These tranches are the safest and receive priority when it comes to cash flow distributions. Because of their lower risk, they offer lower yields.
   - **Mezzanine Tranches**: Positioned in the middle of the risk spectrum, mezzanine tranches offer

moderate risk and yield.

- **Equity Tranches**: These are the riskiest tranches but also have the potential for the highest returns. Investors in equity tranches receive payments only after all other tranches are paid.

The hierarchical structure of tranches, often referred to as a "waterfall," ensures that senior tranche investors are protected from defaults in the underlying loans, while equity tranche investors absorb the majority of the risk.

3. **CLO Manager**:
The CLO manager plays a vital role in the success of the CLO. Their responsibilities include selecting the loans that go into the pool, reinvesting principal payments from maturing loans into new loans, and ensuring the portfolio adheres to regulatory and performance guidelines. An experienced and skilled CLO manager can significantly impact the returns of a CLO.

4. **Cash Flow Waterfalls**:
A critical feature of CLOs is their cash flow waterfall, which determines how cash generated by the underlying loans is distributed among the tranches. Senior tranches are paid first, followed by mezzanine tranches, and finally equity tranches. This prioritization of payments provides protection to senior tranche investors while allowing equity investors to benefit from the residual cash flow.

5. **Credit Enhancements**:
To reduce the risk for investors, CLOs often include credit enhancements such as overcollateralization and interest coverage tests. These mechanisms ensure that the CLO holds more assets than the minimum required to support its liabilities, providing a buffer against potential loan defaults.

Section 3: The Role of CLOs in Modern Finance

CLOs are not just investment vehicles; they are a critical component of the global financial system. They serve as a bridge between borrowers in need of capital and investors seeking higher returns, making them essential to the efficient functioning of credit markets.

1. **Supporting Corporate Borrowing**:
   CLOs provide an avenue for banks to offload corporate loans from their balance sheets, freeing up capital that can be used to make additional loans. This process, known as "credit recycling," ensures that businesses—particularly those with lower credit ratings—have access to the financing they need to grow and expand. Without CLOs, banks would face capacity constraints that could limit lending and slow economic growth.
2. **Diversification and Risk Management**:
   One of the key benefits of CLOs is their ability to diversify risk. By pooling loans from various industries, geographies, and borrowers, CLOs reduce the impact of any single loan default on the overall portfolio. For investors, this diversification helps mitigate risk while providing access to higher-yielding assets.
3. **Resilience in Economic Downturns**:
   CLOs have demonstrated remarkable resilience during periods of economic stress. Even during the 2008 financial crisis, when many structured finance products faced significant losses, senior tranches of CLOs experienced very few defaults. This resilience is largely due to the active management of loan portfolios and the credit enhancements built into CLO structures.
4. **Attracting a Wide Range of Investors**:
   The flexibility of CLOs, with their range of tranches catering to different risk appetites, makes them attractive

to a diverse group of investors. Institutional investors, such as pension funds, insurance companies, and hedge funds, often invest in senior and mezzanine tranches, while equity tranches attract investors seeking higher risk and returns.

5. **Floating Rate Appeal**:
   Another reason CLOs are popular is their floating rate structure, which ties the interest payments from the underlying loans to a benchmark rate (such as LIBOR or SOFR). This feature makes CLOs particularly appealing in rising interest rate environments, as they provide a hedge against inflation and protect investors from interest rate risk.

Chapter 1 lays the foundation for understanding CLO investing by breaking down the basic concepts, components, and importance of CLOs in the financial system. From their unique tranche structure to their role in supporting corporate borrowing and providing diversified investment opportunities, CLOs are a dynamic and powerful tool for investors. As we move into subsequent chapters, we'll dive deeper into the history, structure, risks, and strategies associated with CLOs, equipping you with the knowledge needed to navigate this lucrative yet complex market.

By mastering the fundamentals outlined here, you're already one step closer to becoming an informed and confident CLO investor.

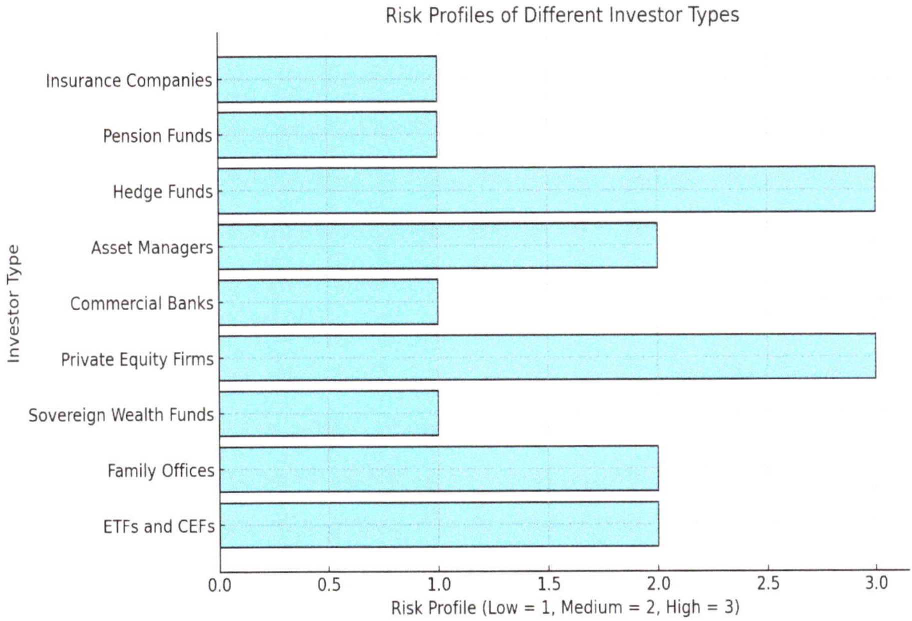

Here's a bar chart showing the risk profiles of different investor types. For investor types with varying risk profiles (like ETFs and CEFs), the average value (2) was used. "CLO Managers" were excluded due to missing data. Let me know if you'd like to modify or add details to the chart!

CHAPTER 2: THE HISTORY AND EVOLUTION OF CLOS

Collateralized Loan Obligations (CLOs) are one of the most sophisticated products in modern financial markets, offering a unique combination of credit diversification and high-yield returns. To fully appreciate their role in today's financial ecosystem, it's essential to understand their historical development. CLOs have evolved significantly since their inception, shaped by economic events, regulatory changes, and investor demand. This chapter will take a deep dive into the history of CLOs, exploring their origins, their growth before and after the 2008 financial crisis, and the pivotal milestones that have defined their evolution.

Section 1: The Origins of CLOs

The story of CLOs begins in the late 1980s and early 1990s when financial institutions started experimenting with new ways to manage risk and free up capital. CLOs emerged as a natural extension of securitization, a process that was already popular in the mortgage market. While mortgage-backed securities (MBS) had been around for decades, CLOs took the basic principles of securitization and applied them to corporate loans.

1. **Securitization Meets Corporate Lending**:
   In the late 1980s, banks faced a challenge: they had significant amounts of corporate loans on their balance sheets, which tied up capital and limited their ability to issue new loans. Regulators, particularly in the United States, had introduced capital adequacy requirements, which meant banks needed to hold substantial reserves against these loans. Securitization provided a solution. By bundling corporate loans into a single investment vehicle and selling the cash flows to investors, banks could remove these loans from their balance sheets and free up capital for additional lending.

The earliest CLOs were relatively small and straightforward. They consisted of pools of loans that were packaged into a single trust, which issued multiple tranches of securities to investors. The senior tranches received first priority on cash flows, while the equity tranches absorbed the residual risk and provided the highest potential returns.

2. **Key Innovations in the 1990s**:
   By the 1990s, CLOs had started gaining traction as investors became more familiar with the concept. Early CLOs were often static, meaning the loan pools were not actively managed. However, as the market matured, active management became a key feature of CLOs. This allowed CLO managers to reinvest cash flows from maturing loans into new loans, enhancing returns and improving portfolio performance.

   Another major innovation during this time was the development of overcollateralization and interest coverage tests, which provided additional safeguards for investors. These mechanisms ensured that CLOs maintained sufficient collateral and cash flow to meet their payment obligations, even in the event of loan defaults.

3. **Early Participants**:
   The early CLO market was dominated by large investment banks and institutional investors. Firms like Drexel Burnham Lambert played a key role in pioneering CLO structures, while institutional investors, such as pension funds and insurance companies, were among the first to recognize the benefits of CLOs as a high-yield investment.

Section 2: The Impact of the 2008 Financial Crisis

The global financial crisis of 2008 was a defining moment for the CLO market. While many structured finance products, such as collateralized debt obligations (CDOs) and mortgage-backed securities (MBS), were at the center of the crisis, CLOs demonstrated surprising resilience. However, the crisis still had a profound impact on the CLO market, leading to regulatory changes and a renewed focus on risk management.

1. **The Collapse of CDOs and the Shadow Over CLOs**: During the financial crisis, collateralized debt obligations (CDOs)—a close cousin of CLOs—were widely blamed for exacerbating the crisis. CDOs, which pooled subprime mortgages and other assets, suffered catastrophic losses as the housing market collapsed. This created a wave of skepticism toward all structured finance products, including CLOs.

   However, unlike CDOs, CLOs performed relatively well during the crisis. The default rates for CLO tranches, particularly senior tranches, remained low, highlighting the robustness of their structure. This resilience helped restore investor confidence in CLOs in the years following the crisis.

2. **Regulatory Changes and Market Adjustments**: In the aftermath of the crisis, regulators introduced sweeping changes aimed at improving transparency and reducing risk in the financial system. These regulations had a significant impact on the CLO market.

   - **Dodd-Frank Act**: The Dodd-Frank Wall Street Reform and Consumer Protection Act, passed in 2010, imposed new requirements on CLO managers and investors. One of the most notable provisions was the "risk retention rule," which required CLO managers to retain at least 5% of the credit risk of the CLO. This rule aligned the interests of CLO managers with those of investors, but it also increased the cost of issuing CLOs.

- **Basel III**: International banking regulations under Basel III introduced higher capital requirements for banks, making it more expensive for banks to hold CLO tranches. This led to a shift in the investor base, with non-bank entities such as hedge funds and private equity firms becoming more prominent players in the CLO market.

3. **Post-Crisis Recovery**:
   Despite the challenges posed by regulatory changes, the CLO market rebounded strongly in the years following the crisis. Investors were drawn to CLOs for their attractive risk-adjusted returns and floating-rate structures, which offered protection against rising interest rates. By the mid-2010s, CLO issuance had reached new heights, with the market evolving into a key component of the global credit ecosystem.

Section 3: Resurgence and Growth in the Post-Crisis Era

The resurgence of CLOs after the 2008 financial crisis marked the beginning of a new era for the market. This period was characterized by innovation, globalization, and increasing investor demand.

1. **Growth of the Global CLO Market**:
   While the CLO market was initially concentrated in the United States, it has since expanded globally. The European CLO market, in particular, has grown significantly, driven by strong demand from institutional investors and favorable regulatory conditions. In recent years, CLO markets in Asia have also begun to emerge, reflecting the increasing globalization of the asset class.

2. **Technological Advancements and Innovation**:
   The post-crisis era has seen the introduction of new technologies and data analytics tools that have transformed

the way CLOs are managed and evaluated. CLO managers now use advanced software and artificial intelligence to monitor loan performance, assess credit risk, and optimize portfolio composition. These innovations have improved the efficiency and transparency of the CLO market, making it more attractive to investors.

3. **Resilience Through Economic Uncertainty**: CLOs have continued to demonstrate resilience in the face of economic uncertainty. During the COVID-19 pandemic, for example, the CLO market experienced some volatility, but it quickly rebounded as central banks implemented monetary stimulus measures. This resilience has reinforced the perception of CLOs as a robust and reliable investment vehicle.

The history of CLOs is a testament to their adaptability and resilience. From their origins in the 1980s to their resurgence in the post-crisis era, CLOs have evolved to meet the changing needs of investors and financial institutions. While the 2008 financial crisis posed significant challenges, it also led to important regulatory reforms and innovations that have strengthened the CLO market.

Today, CLOs are a cornerstone of the global credit market, offering investors a unique combination of diversification, high yields, and risk-adjusted returns. Understanding their history provides valuable insights into their structure, performance, and potential as an investment. As we move forward, the next chapter will take a closer look at the intricate structure of CLOs and the mechanisms that make them such a powerful financial tool.

CHAPTER 3: UNDERSTANDING CLO STRUCTURES

Collateralized Loan Obligations (CLOs) are complex financial instruments, and their structure is the backbone that allows them to offer a unique combination of high yields, diversified exposure, and flexible risk-return profiles. To fully grasp how CLOs work, it is essential to break down their anatomy, cash flow mechanisms, and the operational framework behind them. This chapter will take you on a detailed journey into the intricate structure of CLOs, explaining the purpose and design of their tranches, the concept of cash flow waterfalls, and the legal and operational frameworks that support these vehicles.

Section 1: The Anatomy of a CLO

At the heart of every CLO lies a carefully designed structure that enables it to allocate cash flows from a portfolio of loans to different types of investors based on their risk and return preferences. A CLO can be thought of as a multi-tiered investment vehicle that transforms a pool of corporate loans into tranches of securities with varying levels of risk and reward.

1.1 The Tranche Structure

The core feature of a CLO is its tranche structure, which divides the risk and cash flows from the loan pool into different layers, or "tranches." Each tranche represents a distinct risk-return profile, allowing investors to choose their level of exposure based on their financial goals and risk tolerance.

1. **Senior Tranches**:
    - These are the highest-rated tranches, typically rated AAA or AA by credit rating agencies.
    - Senior tranche investors receive priority in cash flow

distributions, which makes them the safest investment within the CLO structure.
- Because of their lower risk, senior tranches offer lower yields compared to mezzanine or equity tranches.

2. **Mezzanine Tranches**:
    - These tranches sit in the middle of the CLO structure and are rated BBB, BB, or below.
    - Mezzanine investors take on moderate risk and are compensated with higher yields than senior tranche investors.
    - In the event of loan defaults, mezzanine tranches absorb losses only after the equity tranche is fully wiped out, but before the senior tranche is affected.
3. **Equity Tranches**:
    - Equity tranches are unrated and represent the most junior portion of the CLO structure.
    - Investors in the equity tranche are the last to receive payments and are the first to absorb losses from loan defaults.
    - However, they are also entitled to the residual cash flow after all other tranches are paid, offering the potential for significant upside in favorable market conditions.

1.2 Collateral Pool

The collateral pool consists of leveraged loans that serve as the underlying assets of the CLO. These loans are typically issued to companies with below-investment-grade credit ratings (e.g., BB+ or lower). Despite the higher credit risk associated with these loans, they offer higher interest rates, which attract investors seeking yield.

The CLO manager actively manages the collateral pool by buying, selling, and replacing loans to optimize returns and meet performance targets. The diversity of the loan pool—across industries, geographies, and borrowers—helps mitigate risks and enhances the stability of cash flows.

Section 2: Cash Flow Waterfalls and Payment Priorities

The concept of cash flow waterfalls is one of the most critical elements of CLO structures. A CLO waterfall refers to the prioritized order in which cash flows from the collateral pool are distributed among the various tranches of the CLO.

2.1 How Cash Flows Work

When the corporate loans in the collateral pool generate interest and principal payments, these cash flows are collected by the CLO and distributed to tranche holders according to a pre-defined priority structure.

1. **Senior Tranches First**:
    - Investors in the senior tranches receive payments before any other tranche. This priority reduces their risk of loss and ensures a steady stream of income.
2. **Mezzanine Tranches Next**:
    - After senior tranches are fully paid, mezzanine tranche holders receive their payments.
3. **Equity Tranches Last**:
    - The equity tranche receives the residual cash flow after all other tranches are paid. This is why equity tranche holders bear the most risk but have the potential for higher returns.

2.2 Coverage Tests

To protect investors, CLOs include certain coverage tests that ensure the collateral pool generates sufficient cash flow to meet payment obligations. These tests are critical for maintaining the financial integrity of the CLO.

1. **Overcollateralization (OC) Test**:
    - Ensures that the value of the collateral pool exceeds the amount owed to investors. If the test is breached, cash flows are redirected to pay down senior tranches until the test is satisfied.
2. **Interest Coverage (IC) Test**:
    - Ensures that the interest payments from the loan pool are sufficient to cover the interest owed to tranche holders. Breaches in this test also result in cash flow redirection.

2.3 Reinvestment Period

A unique feature of CLOs is the reinvestment period, which typically lasts for the first 3–5 years of the CLO's life. During this period, the CLO manager can reinvest principal payments from maturing loans into new loans, maintaining the size and earning potential of the collateral pool. After the reinvestment period ends, the CLO enters its amortization phase, during which the loan portfolio is gradually liquidated, and cash flows are distributed to investors.

Section 3: Legal and Operational Frameworks

Behind every CLO lies a sophisticated legal and operational framework that ensures its smooth functioning and compliance with regulatory requirements.

3.1 Special Purpose Vehicles (SPVs)

CLOs are typically structured as special purpose vehicles (SPVs), which are standalone legal entities created solely to issue CLO securities. The SPV holds the collateral pool and isolates the CLO's assets from the financial risks of the CLO manager or other entities. This structure provides legal protection for investors, ensuring that their investments are secure even in the event of the manager's insolvency.

3.2 The Role of CLO Managers

CLO managers are responsible for selecting and managing the loans in the collateral pool. Their role includes:

- **Portfolio Construction**: Identifying and acquiring loans that meet the CLO's investment criteria.
- **Active Management**: Monitoring the performance of the loans, replacing underperforming assets, and reinvesting cash flows during the reinvestment period.
- **Compliance**: Ensuring that the CLO complies with its legal, regulatory, and contractual obligations.

The performance of a CLO is heavily influenced by the expertise and strategy of its manager. Experienced managers with a strong track record can enhance returns for investors while minimizing risk.

3.3 Regulatory Considerations

CLOs are subject to a range of regulations designed to promote transparency, protect investors, and maintain financial stability. Some key regulatory frameworks include:

- **Dodd-Frank Act**: Introduced risk retention requirements for CLO managers, aligning their interests with those of investors.
- **Basel III**: Increased capital requirements for banks

holding CLO tranches, impacting their role in the market.

- **European Securitization Regulation**: Governs the issuance and management of CLOs in the European Union, with a focus on risk retention and transparency.

Understanding the structure of a CLO is essential for any investor looking to navigate this complex but rewarding market. The anatomy of CLOs—including their tranche system, collateral pool, and active management—provides investors with a range of options to match their risk-return preferences. The cash flow waterfall ensures a prioritized distribution of payments, while legal and operational frameworks offer robust protections and ensure compliance with regulatory standards.

As you delve deeper into the world of CLO investing, it's important to remember that the structure of a CLO is not static. It evolves over its lifecycle, requiring continuous oversight and analysis. In the next chapter, we'll explore the risks and rewards of CLO investing, diving into the factors that can impact performance and strategies to maximize returns.

CHAPTER 4: RISKS AND REWARDS OF CLO INVESTING

Collateralized Loan Obligations (CLOs) are a popular investment vehicle for institutional and retail investors alike, offering the potential for high yields, diversification, and protection against rising interest rates. However, as with any investment, CLOs are not without risks. Understanding the delicate balance between these risks and rewards is critical for making informed decisions as an investor. In this chapter, we'll take a deep dive into the potential benefits of investing in CLOs, the risks associated with them, and how these risks can be mitigated. By the end of this chapter, you'll have a comprehensive understanding of what makes CLOs both an attractive and a challenging asset class.

Section 1: Key Benefits of CLO Investments

CLOs offer several compelling advantages that have made them a cornerstone of the credit market and a preferred choice for investors seeking risk-adjusted returns. Let's explore the most notable benefits of CLO investing:

1.1 High-Yield Opportunities

One of the primary reasons investors are drawn to CLOs is the potential for higher yields compared to traditional fixed-income securities. CLOs typically invest in leveraged loans, which are loans extended to below-investment-grade companies. These loans carry higher interest rates to compensate for the credit risk, and the income generated from these loans flows through to CLO investors.

- **Senior Tranches**: Even the safest tranches of CLOs, such as AAA-rated senior debt, often offer higher yields than similarly rated corporate bonds or government securities.
- **Mezzanine and Equity Tranches**: These riskier tranches offer significantly higher returns, with equity tranche investors benefiting from residual cash flows after all other obligations are paid.

1.2 Diversification

CLOs provide inherent diversification by pooling loans from a wide range of borrowers, industries, and geographies. This diversification reduces the impact of any single loan default on the overall portfolio.

For example:

- A CLO may hold loans from hundreds of companies across multiple sectors such as healthcare, technology, manufacturing, and retail.
- If one industry faces economic challenges, the

performance of loans in other industries can help stabilize the portfolio.

Diversification within CLOs is particularly beneficial for investors looking to reduce concentration risk in their broader portfolio.

1.3 Floating Rate Exposure

CLOs offer protection against rising interest rates because the underlying leveraged loans are typically structured with floating interest rates. These rates are tied to benchmark rates such as the London Interbank Offered Rate (LIBOR) or the Secured Overnight Financing Rate (SOFR).

When interest rates rise, the income generated by the underlying loans also increases, benefiting CLO investors. This feature makes CLOs an attractive option in environments of tightening monetary policy or rising inflation, where traditional fixed-rate bonds may suffer.

1.4 Resilience During Economic Downturns

Historically, CLOs—particularly their senior tranches—have demonstrated remarkable resilience during periods of economic stress. For example:

- During the 2008 financial crisis, senior CLO tranches experienced far fewer defaults compared to other structured finance products like mortgage-backed securities (MBS) and collateralized debt obligations (CDOs).
- CLO structures include built-in safeguards, such as overcollateralization and interest coverage tests, which provide additional layers of protection for senior investors.

Section 2: Understanding and Mitigating Risks

While CLOs offer many advantages, they are not without risks. Investors must thoroughly understand these risks to make informed decisions and implement strategies to mitigate potential downsides.

2.1 Credit Risk

The underlying loans in a CLO's portfolio are issued to companies with below-investment-grade credit ratings, which inherently carry a higher risk of default. If a borrower defaults on its loan obligations, it can impact the cash flow available to CLO tranche holders.

How Credit Risk is Mitigated:

- Diversification within the CLO portfolio reduces the impact of any single loan default.
- Senior tranche investors are protected by the prioritization of payments in the cash flow waterfall, meaning they are paid first even if some loans default.

2.2 Market Risk and Liquidity Risk

CLOs are subject to market fluctuations that can affect their value, particularly in times of economic uncertainty. Liquidity risk is another concern, as CLOs are less liquid than traditional bonds or stocks. While primary CLO markets are active, the secondary market for CLOs can sometimes experience lower trading volumes, making it challenging to sell positions quickly.

How to Manage Liquidity Risk:

- Investors should focus on tranches that match their investment horizon. For example, equity tranches may require a longer-term commitment, while senior tranches offer more predictable cash flows.

- Diversifying across different CLO managers, issuance dates, and tranche types can help manage liquidity risks.

2.3 Complexity and Transparency Risk

CLOs are highly complex financial instruments, and understanding their structure, cash flow mechanics, and credit enhancements requires significant expertise. Investors who do not fully grasp these intricacies may expose themselves to unintended risks.

How to Address Complexity Risk:

- Partner with experienced financial advisors or asset managers who specialize in CLOs.
- Invest in CLO funds or ETFs, which offer professionally managed exposure to the CLO market without requiring investors to navigate individual deals.

2.4 Regulatory and Legal Risk

The CLO market is subject to a wide range of regulations, including those governing risk retention, reporting standards, and compliance. Changes in regulations can impact the issuance, management, and investment in CLOs.

For instance:

- The Dodd-Frank Act introduced the risk retention rule, requiring CLO managers to retain at least 5% of the credit risk. While this aligns managers' interests with investors, it also increases the cost of issuing CLOs.

How to Stay Ahead of Regulatory Risks:

- Monitor changes in regulatory frameworks, particularly in key markets like the US and Europe.
- Choose CLO managers with strong compliance records and transparency practices.

2.5 Macroeconomic and Interest Rate Risk

While CLOs benefit from rising interest rates due to their floating-rate structure, they can still face challenges during periods of economic recession or extreme volatility. For example:

- If default rates in the underlying loan portfolio rise sharply during a recession, it can impact the performance of CLO tranches, particularly mezzanine and equity tranches.

Section 3: Lessons from Market Cycles

The performance of CLOs during different market cycles provides valuable insights into how they respond to economic downturns, recoveries, and expansions. Examining historical data and case studies can help investors better understand the risks and rewards of CLO investing.

3.1 The Resilience of CLOs During the 2008 Financial Crisis

During the global financial crisis, many structured finance products collapsed, but CLOs—especially their senior tranches—remained resilient. Key reasons include:

- The conservative structure of CLOs, with significant credit enhancements and prioritization of senior tranche payments.
- Diversified loan portfolios that reduced exposure to any single borrower or sector.

However, equity tranche investors experienced significant losses during this period, highlighting the importance of understanding risk allocation in the CLO structure.

3.2 The Rebound of CLOs Post-2008

Following the crisis, the CLO market rebounded strongly, driven by investor demand for high-yield products and the resilience demonstrated by CLOs. Issuance levels surged, and the market adapted to new regulatory requirements.

3.3 Lessons from Recent Economic Events (COVID-19 Pandemic)

The COVID-19 pandemic tested the CLO market once again. While the initial shock caused some volatility, the market quickly stabilized due to government stimulus measures and the floating-rate nature of CLOs, which made them less vulnerable to interest rate fluctuations.

CLO investing offers a compelling mix of high yields, diversification, and floating-rate benefits, making it an attractive option for both institutional and retail investors. However, these rewards come with risks, including credit risk, liquidity challenges, and regulatory uncertainties. To succeed as a CLO investor, it's crucial to thoroughly understand the risks, carefully assess tranche options, and work with experienced managers to navigate the complexities of the market.

By learning from historical market cycles and implementing effective risk management strategies, investors can harness the full potential of CLOs while minimizing potential downsides. As we move into the next chapter, we'll explore the CLO markets and key players, providing an overview of the ecosystem that drives this fascinating asset class.

COLLATERALIZED
LOAN
OBLIGATION
01
?+=!

CHAPTER 5: CLO MARKETS AND KEY PLAYERS

Collateralized Loan Obligations (CLOs) are a vital component of the global credit market, offering a unique opportunity for investors to gain exposure to diversified pools of leveraged loans. The CLO market has grown into a complex ecosystem that spans multiple regions, involves a variety of key players, and includes both primary and secondary markets. This chapter provides a comprehensive overview of the CLO market landscape, diving into its geographic scope, the roles of key participants, and the dynamics of primary and secondary markets. Understanding this ecosystem is essential for navigating the complexities of CLO investing and identifying opportunities in this ever-evolving asset class.

Section 1: Geographic Breakdown of the CLO Market

The CLO market is a global phenomenon, with the United States, Europe, and Asia being the primary regions of activity. While each market operates under a similar structural framework, regional nuances and regulatory environments have led to key differences in market size, growth, and investor preferences.

1.1 The United States: The World's Largest CLO Market

The United States is home to the largest and most mature CLO market, accounting for the majority of global issuance. Some key characteristics of the U.S. CLO market include:

- **Size and Dominance**: The U.S. market accounts for approximately 70-75% of global CLO issuance. In recent years, U.S. CLOs have reached record issuance levels, driven by strong investor demand and the growing pool of leveraged loans.
- **Regulatory Framework**: U.S. CLOs are governed by regulations such as the Dodd-Frank Act, which introduced

the risk retention rule requiring managers to retain at least 5% of the credit risk. This regulation aligns managers' interests with those of investors but also increases the cost of issuance.

- **Floating Rate Loans**: U.S. CLOs primarily invest in floating-rate leveraged loans, making them particularly attractive in rising interest rate environments.

1.2 Europe: A Growing Market with Distinct Characteristics

While smaller than its U.S. counterpart, the European CLO market has seen significant growth in recent years. Some key differences between the U.S. and European CLO markets include:

- **Regulatory Environment**: European CLOs are subject to the European Securitization Regulation (ESR), which imposes strict rules on transparency and risk retention. Unlike the U.S., where the risk retention requirement can be held by the CLO manager, European regulations often require the retention to be held by the originating entity.
- **Loan Features**: European leveraged loans tend to have more borrower-friendly terms, such as "covenant-lite" structures, which lack traditional financial covenants that protect lenders. This can increase risk but also attract investors seeking higher yields.
- **Currency Risk**: Many European CLOs issue securities in euros, but some loans in the collateral pool may be denominated in other currencies, introducing currency risk.

1.3 Emerging Markets: Asia and Beyond

The CLO market in Asia is still in its nascent stages but has shown significant potential for growth. Key factors driving the development of the Asian CLO market include:

- **Growing Corporate Debt Market**: Asia’s rapidly

expanding corporate debt market provides a growing pool of loans that could be securitized into CLOs.

- **Institutional Investor Interest**: Asian institutional investors, such as insurance companies and pension funds, are increasingly exploring CLOs as a high-yield alternative to traditional fixed-income investments.
- **Regulatory Challenges**: A lack of standardization in regulations and legal frameworks across Asian countries has slowed the development of a cohesive CLO market in the region.

Section 2: Key Participants in the CLO Ecosystem

The CLO market is a highly collaborative ecosystem involving a variety of participants, each playing a critical role in the issuance, management, and investment process. Let's take a closer look at the key players in this ecosystem:

2.1 CLO Managers

CLO managers are responsible for selecting, monitoring, and actively managing the loans in the CLO's collateral pool. Their performance is critical to the success of the CLO.

- **Responsibilities**:
  - Constructing the loan portfolio by selecting leveraged loans that meet the CLO's investment criteria.
  - Monitoring loan performance and replacing underperforming loans during the reinvestment period.
  - Ensuring the CLO adheres to regulatory and contractual requirements, such as overcollateralization and interest coverage tests.
- **Top CLO Managers**:

Some of the largest and most reputable CLO managers include Blackstone Credit, PGIM, Carlyle Group, and Apollo Global Management. Investors often evaluate a CLO manager's track record and expertise before investing.

2.2 Institutional Investors

Institutional investors are the primary buyers of CLO securities. Their participation drives demand and liquidity in the market. Common institutional investors include:

- **Pension Funds**: These entities are attracted to senior tranches for their stability and predictable cash flows.
- **Insurance Companies**: Insurance firms favor CLOs for their higher yields compared to corporate bonds, especially in low-interest-rate environments.
- **Hedge Funds and Private Equity Firms**: These investors often focus on mezzanine and equity tranches, seeking higher returns despite the increased risk.

2.3 Rating Agencies

Credit rating agencies such as Moody's, Standard & Poor's (S&P), and Fitch play a pivotal role in the CLO market by assessing the creditworthiness of each tranche.

- **Ratings Process**: Agencies evaluate the credit risk of the collateral pool, the strength of the CLO's structure, and the capabilities of the CLO manager.
- **Investor Confidence**: High credit ratings for senior tranches are critical for attracting institutional investors seeking low-risk assets.

2.4 Investment Banks

Investment banks act as underwriters and arrangers in the CLO issuance process. Their responsibilities include:

- Structuring the CLO and determining the appropriate tranche sizes and risk profiles.
- Marketing the CLO to institutional investors and managing the issuance process.

2.5 Regulatory Bodies

Regulators oversee the CLO market to ensure transparency, stability, and investor protection. Examples include the U.S. Securities and Exchange Commission (SEC), the European Securities and Markets Authority (ESMA), and national regulatory authorities.

Section 3: Primary vs. Secondary CLO Markets

CLOs operate in both primary and secondary markets, each serving a distinct purpose in the lifecycle of a CLO. Understanding these markets is essential for investors looking to buy, sell, or trade CLO securities.

3.1 The Primary CLO Market

The primary market refers to the issuance of new CLOs. Key features include:

- **Issuance Process**: Investment banks structure and underwrite new CLOs, marketing the tranches to institutional investors.
- **Pricing and Demand**: The demand for CLO tranches in the primary market influences their pricing. During periods of strong investor demand, CLO issuers can offer tranches at tighter spreads (lower yields).
- **Reinvestment Period**: New CLOs often include a

reinvestment period, typically lasting 3–5 years, during which the CLO manager can reinvest principal payments into new loans.

3.2 The Secondary CLO Market

The secondary market allows investors to buy and sell existing CLO securities. This market provides liquidity and an opportunity to adjust portfolio allocations. Key considerations include:

- **Liquidity Variations**: Senior tranches tend to be more liquid than mezzanine and equity tranches, which can have limited trading activity.
- **Market Conditions**: The performance of the secondary market is influenced by broader economic conditions, interest rate movements, and credit market trends.
- **Discounts and Premiums**: CLO securities in the secondary market may trade at a discount or premium to their face value, depending on factors such as loan performance and investor sentiment.

3.3 Opportunities in Secondary Trading

Experienced investors often look for opportunities in the secondary market to:

- Purchase CLO tranches at a discount during periods of market dislocation.
- Adjust exposure to specific tranches or CLO managers based on evolving investment strategies.

The CLO market is a dynamic and globally interconnected ecosystem, with the U.S. leading the way in size and influence. Europe is steadily growing, while Asia and other emerging markets are showing signs of development. The success of the CLO market relies on the collaboration of key participants, including CLO managers, institutional investors, rating agencies, and investment banks, each playing a vital role in the lifecycle of a CLO.

Whether you're participating in the primary issuance market or trading in the secondary market, understanding the nuances of CLO markets and the roles of key players is essential for making informed investment decisions. In the next chapter, we'll explore the strategies investors can employ to succeed in the CLO market, from tranche selection to portfolio diversification techniques.

CHAPTER 6: STRATEGIES FOR SUCCESSFUL CLO INVESTING

Collateralized Loan Obligations (CLOs) are a highly attractive investment vehicle, offering a range of opportunities for different types of investors based on their risk tolerance, return expectations, and investment objectives. However, CLO investing requires a strategic approach to navigate the complexities of the market and optimize performance. This chapter provides an in-depth exploration of the various strategies investors can employ to succeed in the CLO market, from selecting the right tranches to managing risk and building diversified portfolios. Whether you are a conservative investor focused on stability or an aggressive investor seeking high returns, this chapter will guide you through actionable strategies tailored to the unique features of CLOs.

Section 1: Choosing the Right Tranches

One of the most critical decisions in CLO investing is selecting the right tranche to match your investment goals and risk tolerance. Each tranche in a CLO structure offers a unique combination of risk, return, and cash flow priorities. Understanding the characteristics of each tranche is essential to making informed investment decisions.

1.1 Senior Tranches (AAA to AA Rated)

Senior tranches are the safest portion of a CLO, offering the highest priority in cash flow distributions and the lowest risk of loss. These tranches are often rated AAA or AA and are suitable for conservative investors seeking stability and predictable income.

Advantages of Senior Tranches:

- **Low Risk**: Senior tranches are highly protected by the CLO structure, receiving payments first and benefiting from overcollateralization and interest coverage tests.
- **Steady Income**: The regular interest payments make senior tranches an attractive option for income-focused investors, such as pension funds and insurance companies.
- **Low Volatility**: Senior tranches are less sensitive to market fluctuations, making them a safer choice during periods of economic uncertainty.

Considerations:

- Lower yields compared to mezzanine or equity tranches due to the reduced risk profile.
- Limited upside potential in favorable market conditions.

1.2 Mezzanine Tranches (BBB to BB Rated)

Mezzanine tranches sit in the middle of the risk spectrum, offering higher yields than senior tranches but also carrying more risk. These tranches are suitable for investors willing to accept moderate risk in exchange for enhanced returns.

Advantages of Mezzanine Tranches:

- **Higher Yields**: Mezzanine tranches offer significantly higher returns compared to senior tranches, making them attractive to yield-seeking investors.
- **Risk-Reward Balance**: These tranches provide a middle

ground between the safety of senior tranches and the high risk of equity tranches.

Considerations:

- Greater sensitivity to defaults in the collateral pool compared to senior tranches.
- Lower cash flow priority, meaning payments could be affected if the collateral pool underperforms.

1.3 Equity Tranches (Unrated)

Equity tranches are the riskiest portion of a CLO structure, offering the potential for high returns but also exposing investors to the greatest risk of loss. Equity investors receive the residual cash flow after all other tranches are paid, making this tranche highly sensitive to the performance of the collateral pool.

Advantages of Equity Tranches:

- **High Potential Returns**: Equity tranches can generate substantial returns in favorable market conditions, particularly when default rates are low, and interest rates are rising.
- **Residual Cash Flows**: Investors benefit from any excess cash flow after other tranches have been paid, providing the opportunity for outsized gains.

Considerations:

- First to absorb losses in the event of loan defaults, making these tranches highly risky.
- Cash flows are unpredictable and heavily influenced by the performance of the CLO manager.

Section 2: Active vs. Passive Investment Approaches

Investors in the CLO market can choose between active and passive investment strategies, depending on their level of expertise, resources, and investment goals. Each approach has its own advantages and challenges.

2.1 Active CLO Investing

Active investing involves directly purchasing individual CLO tranches or managing a portfolio of CLOs to optimize performance. This strategy requires a deep understanding of CLO structures, loan performance, and market dynamics.

Advantages:

- **Customization**: Investors can tailor their portfolios to their specific risk-return preferences by selecting tranches and CLO managers.
- **Opportunity for Alpha**: Active investors can identify undervalued tranches or capitalize on market inefficiencies to generate higher returns.
- **Flexibility**: Active strategies allow investors to adjust their holdings based on market conditions or changing investment goals.

Challenges:

- Requires significant expertise and resources to analyze and manage CLO portfolios effectively.
- Higher transaction costs and management fees compared to passive investing.

2.2 Passive CLO Investing

Passive investing involves gaining exposure to CLOs through pooled investment vehicles such as exchange-traded funds (ETFs), mutual funds, or CLO-focused hedge funds. These vehicles are managed by professionals who handle tranche selection and portfolio construction.

Advantages:

- **Simplicity**: Passive strategies eliminate the need for direct involvement in CLO selection and management.
- **Diversification**: CLO funds typically invest in multiple CLOs, providing broad exposure to the market and reducing concentration risk.
- **Lower Costs**: Management fees for passive funds are generally lower than the costs associated with active investing.

Challenges:

- Limited control over portfolio composition, as investors rely on fund managers to make decisions.
- Returns may be diluted due to the diversification of the fund.

Section 3: Building a Diversified Portfolio

Diversification is a cornerstone of any successful investment strategy, and CLO investing is no exception. By building a diversified portfolio, investors can reduce risk while maximizing the potential for consistent returns. Here's how to achieve diversification in the CLO market:

3.1 Diversify Across Tranches

Investors can achieve a balance between risk and return by allocating their investments across different tranches within the CLO structure.

- **Example Allocation**:
    - 50% in senior tranches for stability.
    - 30% in mezzanine tranches for moderate risk and higher yields.
    - 20% in equity tranches for growth and high-return potential.

This strategy ensures that investors benefit from the stability of senior tranches while participating in the upside potential of riskier tranches.

3.2 Diversify Across CLO Managers

CLO managers play a critical role in the performance of a CLO. Each manager has a unique investment philosophy, expertise, and approach to portfolio construction. By investing in CLOs managed by different managers, investors can reduce the risk associated with poor manager performance.

3.3 Diversify Across CLO Vintages

CLO vintages refer to the year in which a CLO is issued. Market conditions, interest rates, and default rates can vary significantly between vintages, affecting the performance of CLOs issued during different periods.

- Investing across multiple vintages can help investors mitigate the impact of unfavorable market conditions on a single vintage.

3.4 Diversify Across Geographies

The U.S., Europe, and Asia each offer unique opportunities and challenges in the CLO market. Diversifying geographically allows investors to take advantage of regional differences in regulations, loan features, and economic cycles.

CLO investing offers immense potential for returns, but success requires a strategic approach tailored to the unique features of this asset class. Whether you're selecting tranches, choosing between active and passive strategies, or building a diversified portfolio, each decision plays a critical role in determining your overall performance.

By understanding the nuances of CLO structures, tranche characteristics, and market dynamics, investors can position themselves to navigate the complexities of the CLO market and maximize their returns. In the next chapter, we will explore emerging trends and innovations in CLO investing, shedding light on how technological advancements, ESG considerations, and other developments are shaping the future of this dynamic market.

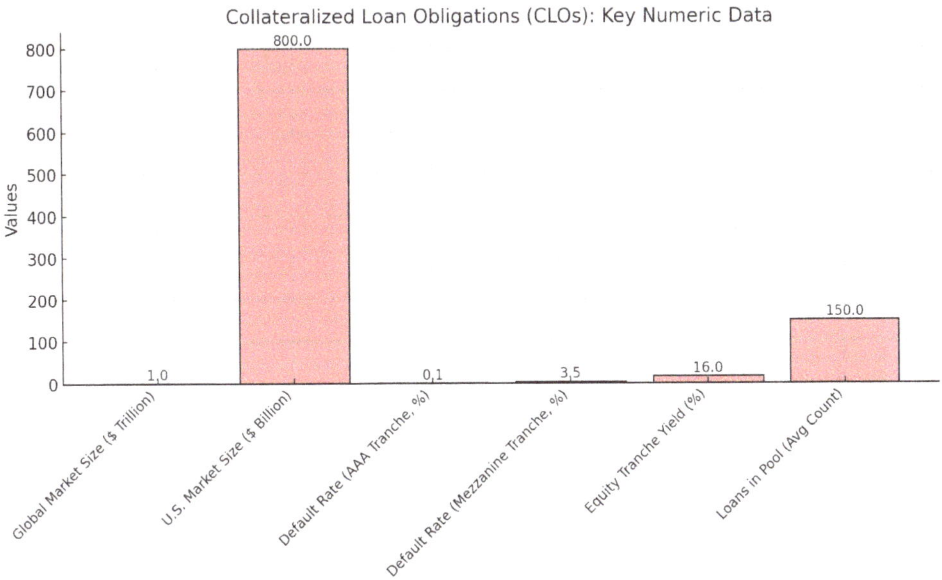

Here's a bar chart displaying key numeric data for Collateralized Loan Obligations (CLOs), including global market size, U.S. market size, default rates, equity tranche yields, and the average number of loans in a pool. Let me know if you'd like to customize or expand it!

CHAPTER 7: EMERGING TRENDS AND INNOVATIONS IN CLO INVESTING

As a dynamic and constantly evolving asset class, Collateralized Loan Obligations (CLOs) have adapted to shifting market conditions, investor preferences, and technological advancements. In recent years, new trends and innovations have emerged, transforming the way CLOs are structured, managed, and perceived by investors. From integrating ESG (Environmental, Social, and Governance) factors into CLO portfolios to leveraging technological tools like artificial intelligence and blockchain, the CLO market is entering an era of rapid change. This chapter explores these emerging trends and innovations, providing a forward-looking view of where CLO investing is headed and how investors can prepare to capitalize on the opportunities ahead.

Section 1: ESG Trends in CLO Issuance and Structuring

In recent years, ESG (Environmental, Social, and Governance) considerations have become a defining trend across global financial markets, including the CLO sector. As investors increasingly demand socially responsible investment opportunities, CLO managers are finding ways to integrate ESG principles into their strategies.

1.1 The Push for ESG-Compliant CLOs

ESG-compliant CLOs are designed to align with investors' ethical and sustainability goals while maintaining the traditional benefits of CLO investing. ESG-compliance can manifest in multiple ways:

- **Exclusionary Screens**: CLO managers exclude loans from companies involved in industries like fossil fuels, weapons manufacturing, tobacco, or other activities deemed harmful to the environment or society.

- **Positive Screening**: CLO managers prioritize loans from companies with strong ESG ratings, such as renewable energy firms or those with excellent governance practices.
- **Sustainability-Linked Loans (SLLs)**: CLOs are increasingly including sustainability-linked loans, which tie the borrower's loan terms (such as interest rates) to meeting predefined ESG performance targets.

1.2 Investor Demand for ESG CLOs

The growth of ESG CLOs is being driven by institutional investors, such as pension funds, insurance companies, and sovereign wealth funds, which are under increasing pressure from stakeholders to invest in assets that align with sustainability goals.

- In Europe, ESG-focused investing has become especially prominent due to regulatory initiatives like the European Union's Sustainable Finance Disclosure Regulation (SFDR).
- In the U.S., while ESG adoption has been slower, demand for ESG-compliant CLOs is steadily rising, particularly among younger and socially conscious investors.

1.3 Challenges of Implementing ESG in CLOs

Despite growing interest, integrating ESG into CLOs comes with challenges:

- **Inconsistent ESG Standards**: A lack of standardization in ESG criteria makes it difficult for CLO managers to evaluate loans consistently.
- **Data Transparency**: Borrowers may not always provide sufficient data to assess their ESG performance.
- **Potential Trade-Offs**: ESG-focused portfolios might exclude high-yield loans, potentially impacting returns for

investors seeking the highest yields.

Section 2: Technology and AI in CLO Portfolio Management

Technology is playing an increasingly significant role in CLO investing, transforming the way managers construct, monitor, and optimize portfolios. From artificial intelligence (AI) to blockchain technology, these tools are improving efficiency, transparency, and performance in the CLO market.

2.1 Artificial Intelligence and Machine Learning

AI and machine learning (ML) have become indispensable tools for CLO managers, enabling them to make data-driven decisions and improve portfolio performance. Key applications include:

- **Loan Selection**: AI algorithms can analyze vast amounts of borrower data to assess creditworthiness and predict default probabilities. By identifying the riskiest loans, CLO managers can avoid potential losses and improve portfolio quality.
- **Risk Monitoring**: AI-powered tools can monitor real-time loan performance, flagging early warning signs of borrower distress, such as missed payments or declining financial metrics.
- **Reinvestment Optimization**: During the reinvestment period, AI can help managers identify the most lucrative opportunities to replace maturing loans while adhering to the CLO's investment criteria.

2.2 Blockchain and Smart Contracts

Blockchain technology has the potential to revolutionize the CLO market by enhancing transparency and operational efficiency.

- **Loan Tracking**: By recording loan-level data on a blockchain, investors can gain real-time visibility into the performance of the underlying collateral pool.
- **Smart Contracts**: CLO payments and compliance tests can be automated using smart contracts, which execute predefined actions (e.g., cash flow distributions) based on blockchain-verified data.
- **Fraud Prevention**: Blockchain's immutable ledger ensures the authenticity of loan data, reducing the risk of fraud or data manipulation.

While blockchain adoption in CLOs is still in its early stages, its potential to improve transparency and reduce administrative costs is gaining attention from market participants.

2.3 Data Analytics for CLO Performance

Advanced data analytics tools are helping investors and managers better understand CLO performance and market dynamics. These tools provide insights into:

- Historical performance trends for CLO managers and tranches.
- Macroeconomic factors, such as interest rate changes, that impact CLO returns.
- Stress testing scenarios to assess how a CLO would perform under adverse conditions.

Section 3: The Evolution of CLO Markets and Investor Preferences

As the CLO market evolves, new trends are reshaping the landscape, from changes in investor preferences to innovative issuance practices. These developments are creating new opportunities and challenges for both managers and investors.

3.1 Growth of Retail Access to CLOs

Historically, CLOs have been the domain of institutional investors due to their complexity and high minimum investment thresholds. However, recent innovations are making CLOs more accessible to retail investors:

- **CLO ETFs and Mutual Funds**: These vehicles allow retail investors to gain exposure to CLOs without directly investing in individual tranches. ETFs, in particular, provide liquidity, transparency, and low management fees.
- **Digital Platforms**: Fintech platforms are beginning to offer fractionalized CLO investments, lowering the entry barriers for smaller investors.

While retail access to CLOs remains limited compared to institutional access, this trend is expected to grow as financial technology continues to evolve.

3.2 Rising Interest Rates and Floating-Rate Appeal

One of the most significant trends impacting the CLO market is the shift toward a rising interest rate environment. CLOs are particularly well-positioned to benefit from this trend due to their floating-rate structure.

- **Impact of Rising Rates**: As benchmark rates like LIBOR or SOFR increase, the interest payments on underlying leveraged loans also rise, boosting cash flow to CLO investors.
- **Investor Appeal**: In periods of rising rates, investors often shift capital away from fixed-rate bonds, which lose value, and into floating-rate assets like CLOs.

3.3 ESG Regulation and Reporting Requirements

Regulators are introducing new rules to ensure greater transparency and standardization in ESG-focused investments.

For example:

- **SFDR (Europe)**: Requires asset managers to disclose the ESG characteristics of their portfolios, including CLOs.
- **U.S. SEC Proposals**: The SEC is exploring enhanced disclosure requirements for ESG funds and structured finance products.

CLO managers will need to adapt to these regulatory changes by improving data collection, reporting, and compliance practices.

3.4 Emergence of CLOs in Emerging Markets

The CLO market is gradually expanding into emerging markets, particularly in Asia. Key drivers include:

- **Demand for Infrastructure Financing**: Emerging economies need significant capital for infrastructure development, creating opportunities for CLOs to securitize loans tied to infrastructure projects.
- **Growing Institutional Investor Base**: As institutional investors in Asia become more sophisticated, they are increasingly exploring CLOs as a high-yield alternative to traditional fixed income.

Challenges in these regions include regulatory fragmentation, currency risk, and a lack of standardized loan documentation. However, the potential for growth remains significant.

The CLO market is evolving rapidly, driven by trends such as ESG integration, technological innovation, and changing investor preferences. These emerging developments are reshaping the way CLOs are structured, managed, and traded, creating both opportunities and challenges for market participants.

Investors who stay ahead of these trends will be well-positioned to capitalize on the future of CLO investing. By incorporating ESG principles, leveraging technological tools like AI and blockchain, and adapting to shifting market conditions, investors can unlock new levels of value in this dynamic asset class.

In the next chapter, we will look to the future of CLO investing, exploring the long-term prospects for this market and the challenges it may face in the years to come. From regulatory developments to macroeconomic trends, Chapter 8 will provide a comprehensive outlook on where the CLO market is headed.

COLLATERALIZED LOAN
OBLIGATION

CHAPTER 8: THE FUTURE OF CLO INVESTING

As the global financial landscape evolves, so too does the market for Collateralized Loan Obligations (CLOs). Having weathered multiple economic cycles and financial crises, CLOs have emerged as one of the most resilient and adaptable asset classes. However, as with any financial instrument, CLOs face both challenges and opportunities in the years ahead. From regulatory changes and technological disruption to shifting investor preferences and macroeconomic trends, the future of CLO investing will be shaped by a variety of factors. In this chapter, we'll explore the long-term outlook for CLOs, identify key challenges and opportunities, and provide insights into how investors can prepare for what lies ahead.

Section 1: Predictions for the Next Decade

1.1 Continued Growth in Global CLO Markets

The CLO market is expected to continue expanding over the next decade, driven by increasing demand for high-yield investment opportunities and the growth of the leveraged loan market.

- **Market Size**: The global CLO market, led by the United States and Europe, is projected to reach new issuance records as institutional investors seek alternatives to traditional fixed-income securities.
- **Regional Expansion**: Emerging markets, particularly in Asia, are expected to contribute to the growth of the global CLO market as corporate debt issuance increases and financial markets mature.
- **Institutional Demand**: Pension funds, insurance companies, and sovereign wealth funds will likely remain the primary drivers of demand for CLOs, especially senior and mezzanine tranches.

1.2 Evolution of CLO Structures

The structure of CLOs will continue to evolve to meet changing market demands and regulatory requirements. Key trends include:

- **ESG Integration**: CLOs will increasingly incorporate ESG principles, with managers tailoring portfolios to meet investor preferences for sustainability and social responsibility.
- **Hybrid Structures**: Innovative CLO structures, such as hybrid portfolios combining leveraged loans with other asset classes (e.g., private credit, middle-market loans), may emerge to attract new types of investors.
- **Shorter Reinvestment Periods**: To adapt to potential changes in interest rates and macroeconomic conditions, CLO managers may begin offering structures with shorter reinvestment periods.

1.3 Rising Popularity of CLO ETFs and Retail Access

The development of exchange-traded funds (ETFs) and mutual funds focused on CLOs is expected to grow, making this asset class more accessible to retail investors. This democratization of access will:

- Provide smaller investors with exposure to CLOs without the need for direct investment in complex tranches.
- Increase market liquidity as more participants enter the secondary market.

Section 2: Challenges Facing the CLO Market

While the future of CLO investing is bright, it is not without significant challenges. The following are some of the major hurdles that the CLO market will face in the coming years:

2.1 Regulatory and Compliance Challenges

The CLO market operates within a highly regulated environment, and changes in regulatory frameworks can have far-reaching implications for issuers, managers, and investors.

- **U.S. Risk Retention Rule**: While some aspects of the Dodd-Frank Act's risk retention requirements have been relaxed, any reintroduction of stricter rules could increase the cost of CLO issuance.
- **European Securitization Regulation (ESR)**: European CLOs face compliance with ESR requirements, which include strict transparency and risk retention standards. Meeting these requirements can be costly and time-consuming.
- **Global ESG Regulation**: As ESG investing becomes more prominent, CLO managers will face increasing pressure to align portfolios with ESG criteria. Regulatory bodies such as the SEC and the European Union are likely to impose stricter disclosure and reporting requirements on ESG-focused CLOs.

2.2 Rising Default Rates in Leveraged Loans

The health of the CLO market is closely tied to the performance of the leveraged loan market. Rising default rates among borrowers could pose risks to CLO performance, particularly for mezzanine and equity tranche investors.

- **Economic Recession**: In the event of a prolonged economic downturn, the default rate on leveraged loans could increase significantly, impacting cash flows to CLO investors.
- **Covenant-Lite Loans**: The growing prevalence of covenant-lite loans, which lack traditional financial protections for lenders, could exacerbate losses during periods of stress.

2.3 Liquidity Challenges in the Secondary Market

Although the CLO secondary market has grown in recent years, it remains less liquid than other asset classes.

- Investors in mezzanine and equity tranches may face challenges in selling their positions quickly during periods of market volatility.
- Regulatory restrictions on bank participation in the secondary market could limit liquidity, especially in times of economic uncertainty.

Section 3: Opportunities for the Future

Despite these challenges, the CLO market presents significant opportunities for innovation, growth, and adaptation to evolving market conditions.

3.1 Adoption of Technology and AI

Technology will play a transformative role in the future of CLO management and investing.

- **AI-Driven Portfolio Management**: CLO managers are increasingly using artificial intelligence to optimize portfolio construction, monitor loan performance, and predict default probabilities.
- **Blockchain and Smart Contracts**: Blockchain technology could enhance transparency and efficiency in the CLO market by enabling real-time tracking of loan performance and automating compliance tests.
- **Data Analytics**: Advanced analytics tools will allow investors to better evaluate CLO performance and assess the impact of macroeconomic trends on their portfolios.

3.2 ESG Opportunities

The integration of ESG principles into CLOs presents both a

challenge and an opportunity.

- CLO managers who successfully incorporate ESG-compliant loans into their portfolios will attract new investors and potentially benefit from favorable pricing.
- As ESG reporting becomes more standardized, it will enhance transparency and make it easier for investors to assess the sustainability of CLO portfolios.

3.3 Expansion into Emerging Markets

Emerging markets represent a significant growth opportunity for the CLO market.

- The expansion of corporate debt markets in Asia, Latin America, and Africa will create new opportunities for CLO issuance.
- Investors seeking diversification and exposure to high-growth regions may increasingly turn to emerging market CLOs.

3.4 Rising Interest Rates and Floating-Rate Structures

CLOs are well-positioned to thrive in a rising interest rate environment due to their floating-rate structures.

- As central banks continue to increase interest rates to combat inflation, CLO investors will benefit from higher coupon payments on the underlying leveraged loans.
- This floating-rate feature makes CLOs an attractive alternative to traditional fixed-income securities, which lose value as interest rates rise.

Section 4: Preparing for the Future as a CLO Investor

To successfully navigate the future of CLO investing, investors must adopt a proactive and forward-looking approach. Here are some key strategies to consider:

4.1 Focus on Manager Selection

The choice of CLO manager can significantly impact portfolio performance.

- Investors should evaluate a manager's track record, expertise, and ability to adapt to changing market conditions.
- Strong CLO managers will be those who can skillfully navigate economic uncertainty, manage ESG integration, and leverage technology to optimize portfolios.

4.2 Diversify Across Tranches, Vintages, and Regions

Diversification remains a cornerstone of successful CLO investing.

- Allocate investments across different tranches (senior, mezzanine, equity) to balance risk and reward.
- Invest in CLOs from multiple vintages to mitigate the impact of market cycles.
- Explore opportunities in emerging markets to benefit from regional growth.

4.3 Stay Ahead of Regulatory Changes

Investors must monitor regulatory developments and assess their potential impact on the CLO market.

- Stay informed about new ESG requirements, changes to risk retention rules, and other compliance measures.
- Work with experienced legal and financial advisors to ensure compliance with evolving regulations.

4.4 Leverage Technology

Investors should embrace technological tools to gain a competitive edge in the CLO market.

- Use AI-driven analytics to evaluate CLO performance and identify trends.
- Monitor real-time loan performance data to assess portfolio health.

The future of CLO investing is bright but will require adaptation to new challenges and opportunities. As the market continues to evolve, driven by technological innovation, ESG integration, and global expansion, investors who stay informed and proactive will be best positioned to capitalize on this dynamic asset class. By focusing on manager selection, embracing diversification, leveraging technology, and staying ahead of regulatory changes, investors can navigate the complexities of the CLO market and achieve long-term success.

As we look ahead, CLOs will remain a vital component of the global financial system, offering high yields, diversification, and resilience to investors. The journey of CLO investing doesn't end here—it's an ongoing process of learning, adapting, and thriving in an ever-changing financial world.

CHAPTER 9: CLO INVESTING CASE STUDIES AND LESSONS FROM THE MARKET

As we have explored throughout this book, Collateralized Loan Obligations (CLOs) are a complex and dynamic asset class. While theoretical knowledge about CLO structures, strategies, risks, and market trends is essential, nothing cements understanding better than examining real-world case studies. These case studies illustrate how CLOs have performed across various economic environments, showcase the decision-making processes of investors and managers, and reveal valuable lessons that can guide future investment strategies. In this chapter, we'll analyze historical examples of CLO performance, break down pivotal moments in the CLO market, and extract actionable insights from both successes and failures.

Section 1: Historical Case Studies of CLO Performance

1.1 CLO Resilience During the 2008 Financial Crisis

The 2008 financial crisis is often seen as the ultimate stress test for structured finance products, with catastrophic losses seen in mortgage-backed securities (MBS) and collateralized debt obligations (CDOs). However, CLOs proved to be a notable exception, particularly senior tranches.

The Situation:

- Leading up to the crisis, the leveraged loan market had grown significantly, fueled by low interest rates and abundant liquidity. CLOs were a major buyer of these loans, which increased the issuance of new CLOs.
- When the financial crisis hit, many corporate borrowers faced financial distress, causing concerns about defaults in leveraged loan portfolios.

CLO Performance:

- Despite fears of mass defaults, the majority of CLOs, especially senior tranches, remained resilient.
    - AAA-rated tranches of CLOs issued before the crisis experienced *zero defaults*.
    - Mezzanine tranches saw some losses, but the severity was much lower compared to other structured products like CDOs.
    - Equity tranches experienced significant volatility and losses, reflecting their higher risk profile.

Lessons Learned:

- **Structural Protections Work**: Features like overcollateralization tests, interest coverage tests, and waterfall payment structures shielded senior investors from losses.
- **Active Management Matters**: Skilled CLO managers were able to replace underperforming loans and stabilize portfolios during the crisis.
- **CLOs Are Different From CDOs**: While both are structured products, CLOs focus on cash-generating corporate loans, whereas CDOs were tied to speculative mortgage-backed securities with far less predictable cash flows.

1.2 Post-Crisis Rebound: The 2010s Boom in CLO Issuance

After the financial crisis, CLOs entered a period of remarkable growth, driven by investors seeking high-yield alternatives in a low-interest-rate environment.

The Situation:

- By 2010, financial markets were stabilizing, and corporate borrowers began accessing credit markets again. Leveraged loan issuance surged, providing ample collateral for new CLOs.
- Investors, wary of MBS and other structured products, turned to CLOs due to their strong performance during the crisis.

CLO Market Performance:

- From 2010 to 2019, CLO issuance skyrocketed, with annual volumes reaching record highs.
- Investors favored senior tranches for their stability, but equity tranches also attracted interest due to their high returns in the post-crisis recovery.

- CLOs issued during this period, often referred to as "CLO 2.0," featured improved transparency, stricter regulatory oversight, and tighter loan covenants compared to pre-crisis CLOs.

Lessons Learned:

- **Investor Confidence Returns**: The strong historical performance of CLOs during the crisis helped rebuild investor trust in the asset class.
- **Regulatory Compliance Is Key**: Changes like the Dodd-Frank risk retention rule and enhanced disclosure requirements improved market transparency and stability.
- **Opportunities in Recovery**: Economic recoveries often present lucrative opportunities for CLO equity investors, as low default rates and rising interest rates boost returns.

1.3 CLOs During the COVID-19 Pandemic (2020)

The COVID-19 pandemic presented a sudden and severe economic shock, raising concerns about the performance of CLOs during a period of extreme uncertainty.

The Situation:

- As the pandemic unfolded, global markets experienced significant volatility. Many industries, such as travel, hospitality, and retail, faced unprecedented challenges, increasing the risk of defaults in leveraged loan portfolios.
- CLO issuance initially slowed as investors assessed the economic impact of the pandemic.

CLO Market Performance:

- CLO senior tranches once again demonstrated resilience, with minimal defaults reported even at the height of the crisis.
- Equity tranches faced significant volatility due to cash

flow disruptions caused by payment deferrals and temporary defaults in the underlying loans.
- By late 2020, the market began to recover as government stimulus measures and central bank interventions stabilized financial markets.

Lessons Learned:

- **Flexibility Is Essential**: CLO managers actively managed portfolios by trading out loans from distressed sectors and reinvesting in stronger credits.
- **Macroeconomic Policy Matters**: Central bank actions, such as interest rate cuts and quantitative easing, played a crucial role in stabilizing the CLO market.
- **CLOs Can Handle Stress**: Despite the economic uncertainty, the CLO market recovered quickly, reaffirming its resilience during periods of crisis.

Section 2: Lessons from Successful CLO Managers

2.1 Case Study: The Role of CLO Managers in Outperforming Portfolios

Top-performing CLO managers often outperform the broader market by implementing specific strategies and demonstrating expertise in portfolio management. Let's examine what sets them apart:

Key Strategies of Top Managers:

- **Loan Selection**: High-performing managers prioritize loans with strong fundamentals, avoiding industries with high volatility or cyclical risks.
- **Active Reinvestment**: During the reinvestment period, skilled managers actively trade maturing loans for higher-quality assets or loans with better spreads.
- **Adapting to Trends**: Leading managers stay ahead of

market trends, such as ESG integration, and align portfolios with investor preferences.

Example:
Blackstone Credit, one of the largest CLO managers, has consistently delivered strong returns by leveraging its extensive credit research capabilities and focusing on diversified portfolios. Their expertise in navigating market cycles has allowed them to outperform peers, particularly in volatile environments.

Lesson:

- **Manager Selection Is Critical**: Investors should evaluate a CLO manager's track record, loan selection criteria, and ability to adapt to market conditions.

Section 3: Common Mistakes and Pitfalls in CLO Investing

3.1 Ignoring Tranche Risk

Many investors are attracted to the high yields of mezzanine and equity tranches but fail to fully appreciate the risks involved.

Example:

- During the 2008 financial crisis, some mezzanine and equity investors experienced significant losses due to rising defaults in leveraged loan portfolios.

Lesson:

- **Understand the Risk-Return Tradeoff**: Investors must carefully assess their risk tolerance before investing in mezzanine or equity tranches and should consider diversifying across tranches to mitigate losses.

3.2 Overconcentration in One Manager or Vintage

Overreliance on a single CLO manager or concentrating

investments in a specific vintage can expose investors to unnecessary risk.

Example:

- Investors who concentrated in CLO vintages issued in 2006-2007 (pre-crisis) experienced higher losses due to deteriorating loan quality and macroeconomic conditions.

Lesson:

- **Diversify Investments**: Spread investments across multiple CLO managers, vintages, and geographies to reduce concentration risk.

3.3 Underestimating Liquidity Challenges

Some investors fail to account for the relative illiquidity of CLOs, particularly mezzanine and equity tranches in the secondary market.

Lesson:

- **Plan for the Long Term**: CLOs, especially equity tranches, are best suited for long-term investors who can hold through periods of volatility.

The history of CLO investing is filled with valuable lessons for investors, ranging from the importance of manager selection and tranche diversification to the resilience of the CLO market during periods of stress. By examining past successes and failures, investors can better understand how to navigate the complexities of CLO investing and position themselves for long-term success.

As we have seen through these case studies, CLOs have consistently proven to be a robust and resilient asset class, even in the face of economic crises. However, success in CLO investing requires careful analysis, a forward-looking approach, and an understanding of the risks involved. By applying the lessons from past market experiences, investors can confidently navigate the evolving CLO market and achieve their investment objectives.

CHAPTER 10: MASTERING CLO INVESTING – A COMPREHENSIVE GUIDE TO LONG-TERM SUCCESS

As we conclude this book, it is vital to bring together the knowledge and strategies we've explored throughout the previous chapters and distill them into actionable steps for mastering CLO (Collateralized Loan Obligations) investing. The CLO market is a highly rewarding yet intricate asset class, requiring a combination of technical expertise, sound risk management, and an ability to adapt to changing market dynamics. While CLOs offer unparalleled opportunities for yield, diversification, and floating-rate exposure, their complexity and evolving nature mean that success is reserved for well-informed, disciplined investors.

This chapter provides a practical roadmap for long-term success in CLO investing. From choosing the right strategies and managing risk to understanding key performance metrics and adapting to future trends, we'll explore how to apply what you've learned in the real world. By mastering the following principles, you'll be equipped to thrive in this dynamic market.

Section 1: Building a Strong Foundation for CLO Investing

Before diving into the intricacies of CLO investments, it's important to establish a strong foundation by understanding the essential concepts and setting clear objectives.

1.1 Defining Your Investment Objectives

CLOs offer different risk-return profiles depending on the tranche you choose. Your first step should be to define your investment goals and align them with the appropriate CLO investment strategy:

- **Conservative Income Goals**: Focus on AAA- or AA-rated senior tranches for low-risk, steady income.
- **Balanced Growth and Yield**: Consider mezzanine tranches (BBB or BB-rated) that balance moderate risk with higher returns.
- **High-Risk, High-Reward Objectives**: Invest in equity tranches for the potential of significant upside but with the understanding of high risk and volatility.

By defining your goals upfront, you'll avoid the common mistake of chasing returns without fully understanding the associated risks.

1.2 Gaining a Deep Understanding of CLO Structures

Mastery of CLO investing begins with a thorough understanding of the underlying structure, including:

- The **tranche hierarchy** and how it allocates risk and return.
- The **cash flow waterfall**, which dictates the order in which payments are distributed.
- **Credit enhancements**, such as overcollateralization and interest coverage tests, that protect senior tranche investors.

Investing without this knowledge can lead to poor decision-making, particularly when selecting tranches or evaluating CLO managers.

1.3 Identifying Key Metrics for Evaluating CLOs

Investors must become proficient in interpreting the key performance metrics that determine the health and attractiveness of a CLO, such as:

- **Default Rates**: The percentage of loans in the CLO portfolio that have defaulted. Lower default rates indicate stronger portfolio performance.

- **Weighted Average Life (WAL)**: The average time it takes for the principal of loans in the portfolio to be repaid. Shorter WALs are less sensitive to market conditions.
- **Weighted Average Spread (WAS)**: The average interest spread of the loans over a benchmark (e.g., LIBOR). Higher WAS indicates a greater potential for yield.
- **Equity Internal Rate of Return (IRR)**: The projected return for equity tranche investors, which depends heavily on loan performance and prepayment rates.

Understanding these metrics will allow you to evaluate and compare CLO investments effectively.

Section 2: Developing a Winning CLO Investment Strategy

2.1 Diversification: The Cornerstone of Risk Management

Diversification is one of the most effective ways to manage risk in the CLO market. A well-diversified CLO portfolio minimizes the impact of defaults and market volatility. Consider diversifying across the following dimensions:

- **Tranche Types**: Spread investments across senior, mezzanine, and equity tranches to achieve a balanced risk-return profile.
- **CLO Managers**: Invest in CLOs managed by different managers to mitigate the risk of poor performance from a single manager.
- **Geographies**: Explore opportunities in U.S., European, and emerging market CLOs to benefit from regional differences in economic cycles and regulations.
- **Vintages**: Allocate investments across different issuance years to avoid overexposure to loans originated during a single economic environment.

2.2 Combining Active and Passive Approaches

While CLO investing is often associated with active management, passive investment options such as CLO-focused ETFs and mutual funds are growing in popularity.

- **Active Investing**: Provides flexibility to select specific CLO tranches, tailor portfolios, and capitalize on market inefficiencies.
- **Passive Investing**: Offers diversification and simplicity by giving investors exposure to a broad portfolio of CLOs without the need for individual tranche selection.

Many investors find success by combining the two approaches—actively managing high-conviction positions while using passive funds for broad market exposure.

2.3 Adapting to Market Cycles

CLO performance is influenced by macroeconomic conditions, including interest rates, default rates, and credit spreads. Adapting your strategy to market cycles can improve returns:

- **In Rising Rate Environments**: Favor floating-rate CLO tranches, as higher benchmark rates increase the income generated by the underlying loans.
- **In Recessions**: Prioritize senior tranches, which are less vulnerable to defaults and provide greater stability.
- **During Market Recoveries**: Consider equity tranches, which can deliver outsized returns when default rates decline and loan prepayment activity accelerates.

Section 3: Risk Management for Long-Term Success

While CLOs are designed with structural protections, they still carry significant risks. A successful investor must have a clear risk management strategy to minimize potential losses.

3.1 Managing Credit Risk

Credit risk arises from defaults in the underlying loan portfolio. To mitigate credit risk:

- Invest in CLOs with strong credit enhancement features, such as high overcollateralization ratios.
- Focus on CLO managers with a track record of selecting high-quality loans.
- Monitor the performance of industries represented in the collateral pool, avoiding sectors with high cyclicality or structural decline.

3.2 Understanding Liquidity Risk

CLOs, particularly mezzanine and equity tranches, are less liquid than traditional fixed-income securities. To manage liquidity risk:

- Avoid overconcentration in tranches that may be difficult to sell during periods of market stress.
- Align your investment horizon with the expected cash flow timeline of the CLO. For example, equity tranches require a longer-term commitment.
- Maintain a portion of your portfolio in more liquid investments to meet short-term cash needs.

3.3 Monitoring Manager Risk

The performance of a CLO is heavily dependent on the expertise of its manager. Regularly evaluate your CLO manager based on:

- Loan default rates in their portfolios compared to industry benchmarks.
- Reinvestment decisions and their impact on portfolio quality.
- Transparency and reporting practices.

Section 4: Preparing for the Future of CLO Investing

4.1 Staying Ahead of Regulatory Changes

Regulations governing CLOs are constantly evolving, particularly as ESG considerations and transparency requirements become more prominent. Stay informed by:

- Regularly reviewing updates from regulatory bodies such as the SEC (U.S.) and ESMA (Europe).
- Partnering with legal and financial advisors to ensure compliance with new rules.
- Monitoring how regulatory changes impact issuance trends and investor demand.

4.2 Leveraging Technology and Data Analytics

Technology will play an increasingly important role in CLO investing. Embrace tools such as:

- **AI-Powered Analytics**: Use AI to identify undervalued tranches, predict defaults, and optimize portfolio allocations.
- **Blockchain for Transparency**: As blockchain adoption grows, investors will gain access to real-time loan performance data, improving decision-making.
- **Automated Risk Monitoring**: Leverage software that tracks key metrics, such as overcollateralization ratios, and provides early warnings for potential breaches.

4.3 Embracing ESG Opportunities

The integration of ESG principles into CLOs is no longer optional—it's a necessity for attracting institutional capital. Prepare by:

- Evaluating the ESG criteria of loans in CLO portfolios.

- Engaging with CLO managers who have strong ESG policies and reporting capabilities.
- Staying informed about global ESG regulations, such as the EU's Sustainable Finance Disclosure Regulation (SFDR).

Becoming a Master of CLO Investing

Mastering CLO investing requires a combination of technical expertise, strategic thinking, and adaptability. By applying the lessons from this book, you will be better prepared to navigate the complexities of the CLO market and seize opportunities for long-term success. Whether you are a conservative investor seeking stability or a bold investor pursuing high returns, the principles outlined in this chapter will serve as your roadmap to achieving your financial goals in the CLO space.

CLOs represent an exciting and dynamic asset class, offering unmatched opportunities for yield, diversification, and protection against rising interest rates. With careful planning, disciplined risk management, and a willingness to adapt to change, you can confidently thrive in this unique market. The journey to mastering CLO investing begins with knowledge, but success comes from putting that knowledge into action. Your next step is to dive into the market, armed with the tools and insights you've gained, and begin building your path to financial success through CLOs.

CHAPTER 11: COLLATERALIZED LOAN OBLIGATION (CLO) STRUCTURE

A **Collateralized Loan Obligation (CLO)** is a structured financial product that pools together a portfolio of loans (mainly leveraged loans) and divides them into different **tranches**. Each tranche represents a different level of risk, return, and claim on the cash flows generated by the loan pool. Here's an in-depth breakdown of the CLO structure with numeric data:

1. The CLO Asset Pool (Underlying Loans):

A CLO typically contains a pool of **100 to 200** loans with an aggregate value ranging from **$300 million to $1 billion** or more. The loans in the CLO are primarily **leveraged loans** — corporate loans to businesses with credit ratings below investment grade.

- **Typical Loan Size**: Loans within the pool are often between **$10 million to $100 million** each.
- **Number of Loans**: The pool generally contains **100 to 200 loans** across different industries (e.g., technology, healthcare, energy, consumer products).
- **Diversification**: The loan pool is highly diversified, with no single loan typically representing more than **1-2%** of the total pool value.

2. CLO Tranches:

The CLO is structured with different tranches, which are ranked by seniority. These tranches are sold to investors, with higher-ranked tranches receiving payments first, and lower-ranked tranches being paid later. The CLO structure typically consists of:

- **Senior Tranches**: Represent about **60-80%** of the CLO's total value and are the least risky.

- **Mezzanine Tranches**: Represent about **10-20%** of the CLO's total value and offer higher yields than senior tranches.
- **Equity Tranches**: Represent about **5-10%** of the CLO's value and carry the highest risk but offer the highest potential return.

3. CLO Tranche Breakdown:

Senior Tranches (AAA, AA, A, BBB):

- **AAA Tranches**: Typically the highest-rated tranches, they represent **30-40%** of the CLO's total value. These tranches receive the first priority in cash flow payments and are considered the least risky.
    - **Yield**: 3-5% annually.
    - **Rating**: Investment grade (AAA, AA, A).
- **AA to BBB Tranches**: These represent the next 30-40% of the CLO's value. They offer higher yields than AAA tranches but come with greater risk.
    - **Yield**: 4-6% annually.
    - **Rating**: Investment-grade (BBB).

Mezzanine Tranches (BB, B):

- **BB Tranches**: These are higher-risk tranches, offering higher returns, typically representing **15-20%** of the CLO's value.
    - **Yield**: 6-8% annually.
    - **Rating**: Below investment grade (BB).
- **B Tranches**: These are even riskier, providing higher yields, and represent about **5-10%** of the CLO's total value.

- **Yield**: 8-10% annually.
- **Rating**: Below investment grade (B).

Equity Tranches:

- **Equity Tranches**: Represent the riskiest portion of the CLO, typically around **5-10%** of the total CLO value. These tranches are paid last, after all senior and mezzanine tranches have been paid.
    - **Yield**: Potentially **8-15%** annually, depending on the performance of the underlying loans. In return, investors in the equity tranche bear the first losses from loan defaults.
    - **Rating**: Typically unrated due to the high risk of loss.

4. Cash Flow Waterfall:

The CLO operates under a **cash flow waterfall** structure, meaning payments from the underlying loans are distributed according to the hierarchy of tranches.

1. **Interest Payments**: The interest income from the underlying loans is distributed starting with the senior tranches. For example, if the CLO generates **$50 million** in interest income in a given period, the distribution might look like:
    - **Senior Tranches (AAA, AA, A)**: Receive the first **$35 million** (70%).
    - **Mezzanine Tranches (BB, B)**: Receive the next **$10 million** (20%).
    - **Equity Tranches**: The remaining **$5 million** (10%) goes to the equity investors.
2. **Principal Payments**: Similarly, any principal repayments are distributed in the same order of seniority, with senior tranches receiving the first payouts.

3. **Excess Cash Flows**: If there are any remaining funds after the senior and mezzanine tranches are paid, the excess cash flows go to the equity tranche. These are the residual payments that reflect the CLO's overall performance.

5. CLO Structural Features:

- **Overcollateralization (OC) Tests**: This ensures that the CLO's assets exceed the liabilities by a required margin. Typically, the **OC ratio** needs to stay above **130-140%** to avoid triggering default provisions.
- **Interest Coverage (IC) Tests**: The CLO must maintain a minimum interest coverage ratio (typically around **2x to 2.5x**) to ensure it can meet its interest payments to investors.
- **Reinvestment Period**: Generally lasts **4-5 years**. During this period, the CLO manager can reinvest the proceeds from loan repayments into new loans to maintain the value of the CLO portfolio.
- **Amortization Period**: After the reinvestment period, the CLO enters an **amortization phase** where no new loans are purchased, and principal payments are used to pay down the tranches.

CLO Tranches by Risk and Return (Numeric Summary):

Tranche Type	Risk Level	Yield/Return	Typical Allocation	Rating	Payment Priority
Senior (AAA, AA, A, BBB)	Low	3-6% annually	60-80% of CLO value	Investment grade	Paid first
Mezzanine (BB, B)	Medium	6-10% annually	10-20% of CLO value	Below investment grade	Paid after senior

Tranche Type	Risk Level	Yield/Return	Typical Allocation	Rating	Payment Priority
Equity	High	8-15% annually	5-10% of CLO value	Not rated	Paid last

The **CLO structure** is designed to offer a wide range of risk-return profiles, from safer senior tranches to the higher-risk equity tranches. Senior tranches typically make up **60-80%** of the CLO's value and offer yields ranging from **3-5%**, while equity tranches represent **5-10%** of the CLO value but offer returns of **8-15%**, albeit with much higher risk. Investors in CLOs must carefully assess their risk tolerance and understand how CLOs distribute cash flows, particularly during the reinvestment and amortization periods, to fully evaluate the potential returns and risks of each tranche.

CHAPTER 11 : COLLATERALIZED LOAN OBLIGATION & ETF

-Loan ETF

A Loan ETF (Exchange-Traded Fund) is an investment fund that holds a portfolio of loans, typically leveraged loans or syndicated loans. These loans are often issued by companies with lower credit ratings, and they have floating interest rates that are typically tied to benchmarks such as LIBOR (London Interbank Offered Rate) or SOFR (Secured Overnight Financing Rate). Loan ETFs provide investors with exposure to these loans through a single traded security, which can offer higher yields compared to traditional bonds, while also providing diversification and liquidity.

Loan ETFs typically invest in **senior secured loans**, which are loans made to corporations that are secured by collateral. These loans have priority over unsecured loans and are considered safer than high-yield bonds. However, they still carry risks, such as credit risk, interest rate risk, and liquidity risk.

Key Features of Loan ETFs:

1. **Diversification:**
    - Loan ETFs typically hold a large number of loans from various industries, which helps spread risk across different borrowers and sectors. This diversification reduces the impact of any single default or credit event on the overall performance of the ETF.
2. **Floating Interest Rates:**
    - The loans held in a Loan ETF are typically **floating-rate instruments**, meaning their interest payments adjust based on changes in benchmark rates like LIBOR or SOFR. As a result, Loan ETFs can offer some protection against rising interest rates, as the

coupon payments on the underlying loans tend to increase when interest rates rise.

3. **Liquidity:**
    - One of the primary advantages of Loan ETFs is their **liquidity**. Unlike individual loans, which can be difficult to buy and sell on the secondary market, Loan ETFs can be traded on stock exchanges just like stocks, providing daily liquidity to investors.
4. **Yield Potential:**
    - Loan ETFs can offer attractive yields compared to traditional fixed-income investments, such as government bonds or investment-grade corporate bonds. This is because leveraged loans often pay higher interest rates to compensate for the higher risk associated with the borrowers.
5. **Lower Credit Quality:**
    - Many of the loans in Loan ETFs are made to companies with lower credit ratings (i.e., **sub-investment grade** or **junk-rated** companies). As a result, these loans carry **credit risk**, as borrowers may be more likely to default on their debt obligations.

Popular Loan ETFs:

1. **Invesco Senior Loan ETF (BKLN):**
    - **Focus**: Invests in senior secured loans, primarily to below-investment-grade companies.
    - **Yield**: Approximately **3-4%** annually, depending on interest rate changes.
    - **Expense Ratio**: **0.65%**.
    - **Risk Profile**: Moderate risk due to exposure to loans with lower credit ratings.

2. **SPDR Blackstone Senior Loan ETF (SRLN):**
   - **Focus**: Invests in senior loans to companies, with an emphasis on diversified sectors.
   - **Yield**: Typically yields **4-5%** annually, offering potential income in rising interest rate environments.
   - **Expense Ratio**: **0.70%**.
   - **Risk Profile**: Similar to other loan ETFs, it carries credit risk but offers protection against rising interest rates due to floating-rate loans.
3. **VanEck Vectors Floating Rate High Yield ETF (FLOA):**
   - **Focus**: This ETF invests in floating-rate, high-yield loans, including senior loans to high-risk companies.
   - **Yield**: Historically around **3-5%**, but can fluctuate depending on interest rates and credit spreads.
   - **Expense Ratio**: **0.35%**.
   - **Risk Profile**: Higher yield potential, but increased risk due to the lower credit quality of the loans.

Advantages of Loan ETFs:

1. **Diversified Exposure to Loans**:
   - Loan ETFs allow investors to gain exposure to a broad basket of loans, reducing the impact of any single borrower's default.
2. **Protection Against Rising Interest Rates**:
   - Since loan ETFs typically invest in floating-rate loans, they tend to benefit from rising interest rates. As rates rise, the interest payments on these loans generally increase, providing higher income to investors.
3. **Accessibility**:
   - Loan ETFs are traded on major stock exchanges,

providing a liquid, low-barrier way for retail investors to gain exposure to the loan market, without needing to directly invest in individual loans or manage loan portfolios.

4. **Higher Yield Potential**:
    - Loan ETFs generally offer higher yields compared to traditional fixed-income assets such as government or investment-grade corporate bonds, attracting income-seeking investors.

Disadvantages and Risks of Loan ETFs:

1. **Credit Risk**:
    - Since many of the loans in Loan ETFs are made to companies with lower credit ratings, there is a risk of default. If the borrowers fail to meet their obligations, the ETF's performance may suffer.
2. **Interest Rate Risk**:
    - Although Loan ETFs benefit from rising interest rates, they can still be affected by changes in benchmark rates. If rates rise too quickly or too significantly, borrowers may face challenges in servicing their debt, which could lead to defaults or lower recoveries.
3. **Liquidity Risk**:
    - Although Loan ETFs are traded on stock exchanges, the underlying loans themselves can be less liquid, particularly in times of market stress. If a significant number of loans within the ETF experience difficulties, it could be harder to sell off the ETF holdings quickly.
4. **Economic and Market Conditions**:
    - Loan ETFs are susceptible to the broader economic

environment. In times of economic downturn or recession, the risk of defaults increases, which can negatively impact the performance of the ETF.

Loan ETFs provide investors with an opportunity to gain exposure to floating-rate, senior-secured loans in a diversified and liquid manner. They offer attractive yields, particularly in rising interest rate environments, and help mitigate interest rate risk. However, they also come with credit risk, interest rate risk, and liquidity risk, especially if the underlying borrowers are in financial distress. Investors should weigh the risks and benefits carefully to determine if Loan ETFs align with their investment objectives and risk tolerance.

What is Collateralized Loan Obligation (CLO) ETF ?

A **Collateralized Loan Obligation (CLO) ETF** is an exchange-traded fund that invests in CLOs or CLO-related securities, offering investors a way to gain exposure to this asset class without directly purchasing individual CLO tranches. CLO ETFs typically invest in a diversified portfolio of CLOs or the senior, mezzanine, and sometimes equity tranches of CLO securities, providing exposure to corporate loans, often in the **leveraged loan market**.

Key Features of CLO ETFs:

1. **Diversified Exposure to CLOs**: CLO ETFs typically hold a basket of CLO securities, providing diversification across multiple CLOs and loans. This diversification helps spread the risk inherent in individual loans or tranches.
2. **Tranche Exposure**: CLO ETFs may invest in different tranches, including:
    - **Senior Tranches (AAA, AA, A)**: These are the safest but usually offer lower yields.
    - **Mezzanine Tranches (BB, B)**: These offer higher

yields but come with greater risk.
    - **Equity Tranches**: The riskiest tranches, offering potentially high returns but subject to first losses.
3. **Liquidity**: CLO ETFs offer liquidity, as they can be traded on stock exchanges just like stocks, unlike direct investments in CLOs, which can be less liquid. This makes CLO ETFs a more accessible investment vehicle for retail investors who may want exposure to CLOs but don't have the capacity or desire to directly invest in individual CLO tranches.
4. **Exposure to Floating Rate Debt**: CLOs typically invest in loans with floating interest rates, which means they can benefit from rising interest rates. As a result, CLO ETFs may be appealing in environments where interest rates are expected to increase, as their underlying loans may generate higher yields when rates rise.
5. **Risk and Return Profile**: CLO ETFs, like CLOs, are considered higher risk compared to traditional investment-grade bonds. However, they offer potentially higher yields. The risk in CLO ETFs arises from:
    - **Credit Risk**: The risk of defaults in the underlying leveraged loans.
    - **Interest Rate Risk**: CLOs are sensitive to interest rate movements, as they invest in floating-rate loans.
    - **Market Risk**: The performance of CLO ETFs can be influenced by broader market conditions, such as economic cycles, defaults, and credit spreads.
6. **Fees and Expenses**: CLO ETFs typically have lower fees than actively managed CLO funds or direct investments in CLO tranches. However, the expense ratio can vary depending on the specific ETF.

Popular CLO ETFs:

Several ETFs focus on CLOs or CLO-related securities, each with varying strategies, risk exposures, and yield targets. Some of the most popular CLO ETFs include:

1. **Invesco Senior Loan ETF (BKLN)**:
    - **Focus**: Although it primarily invests in senior loans (including CLOs), BKLN provides indirect exposure to CLOs by investing in leveraged loans that are often part of CLO portfolios.
    - **Yield**: Approximately **3-4%**, depending on market conditions.
    - **Expense Ratio**: Around **0.65%**.
    - **Risk**: Offers exposure to senior loans with lower credit risk compared to mezzanine or equity CLO tranches, but still subject to credit and interest rate risk.
2. **Xtrackers USD High Yield Corporate Bond ETF (HYLB)**:
    - **Focus**: This ETF holds a mix of high-yield bonds, including those backed by leveraged loans. While not a pure CLO ETF, it may provide some indirect exposure to CLOs through its bond holdings.
    - **Yield**: Around **5-6%** annually.
    - **Expense Ratio**: Around **0.20%**.
    - **Risk**: It focuses on higher-yielding bonds, meaning it carries greater risk, including credit risk and interest rate risk.
3. **VanEck Vectors CLO ETF (CLOX)**:
    - **Focus**: A pure CLO ETF, CLOX invests in a portfolio of CLOs, targeting primarily senior and mezzanine CLO tranches.
    - **Yield**: The yield can vary but is often in the **4-6%** range, depending on the mix of tranches and market

conditions.

- **Expense Ratio**: **0.45%**.
- **Risk**: CLOX offers exposure to CLOs and can carry higher risks, particularly if it holds lower-rated tranches like BB or equity tranches.

Advantages of Investing in CLO ETFs:

1. **Diversification**:
    - CLO ETFs provide broad diversification across various loans and industries, reducing the risk of exposure to a single company or sector. This is particularly important since CLOs pool hundreds of loans across many borrowers.
2. **Liquidity**:
    - CLO ETFs trade on exchanges like stocks, making them highly liquid and easily accessible for retail investors. This is in contrast to direct CLO investments, which may have limited liquidity.
3. **Accessibility**:
    - Retail investors can easily access CLO exposure without the need to directly purchase CLO tranches or deal with the complexities of the CLO market.
4. **Yield Potential**:
    - CLO ETFs can offer higher yields than traditional investment-grade bonds or government securities, particularly for those willing to accept additional risk.
5. **Interest Rate Sensitivity**:
    - CLO ETFs can benefit from rising interest rates since most CLOs invest in floating-rate loans. This makes them attractive in an environment where rates are expected to rise.

Disadvantages and Risks of CLO ETFs:

1. **Credit Risk**:
    - CLO ETFs are subject to credit risk, as they invest in leveraged loans that are often made to companies with lower credit ratings. If these companies default, the performance of the CLO may suffer, affecting ETF returns.
2. **Interest Rate Risk**:
    - While CLOs are floating-rate instruments and may benefit from rising rates, CLO ETFs still carry some interest rate risk, especially if the overall rate environment becomes volatile.
3. **Market Risk**:
    - Like all ETFs, CLO ETFs are exposed to market risk, meaning their value can fluctuate with broader market trends, including economic downturns or crises that lead to higher default rates in the underlying loans.
4. **Liquidity Risk**:
    - Although CLO ETFs are liquid, the underlying CLOs can be less liquid, especially those in the lower tranches or during times of market stress.

CLO ETFs provide an accessible way for investors to gain exposure to the potentially high-yielding CLO market without having to deal with the complexities of investing in individual CLO tranches. They offer diversification, liquidity, and the potential for higher returns, particularly in rising interest rate environments. However, investors should be aware of the inherent risks, including credit risk, interest rate risk, and market risk, and ensure that the ETF aligns with their risk tolerance and investment objectives.

-Collateralized Loan Obligation (CLO) and Legal Risks

Investing in **Collateralized Loan Obligations (CLOs)** can expose investors to various legal risks, stemming from the complex structure of CLOs, the underlying assets, and the regulatory environment. Below are some of the key legal risks associated with CLO investing:

1. Credit Risk and Default Risk in the Loan Pool

- **Loan Defaults**: CLOs are backed by pools of corporate loans, many of which are leveraged loans to companies with lower credit ratings. If a significant portion of the loans in the CLO pool defaults, it can result in significant losses for investors, particularly those in junior tranches (such as the equity tranche).
- **Legal Risk of Enforcing Loan Terms**: When loans default or when there is a restructuring, the CLO manager must work through legal mechanisms to recover funds. These processes can be time-consuming, expensive, and may not fully recover the value of the loans, affecting the overall performance of the CLO.
- **Covenant Lite Loans**: Many of the loans in CLOs are "covenant-lite" loans, which have fewer protective covenants for investors. This increases the risk that the borrower may not meet certain financial obligations, potentially resulting in defaults or more challenging restructuring negotiations.

2. Regulatory Risk and Compliance Issues

- **Changes in Regulations**: CLOs are subject to regulatory oversight, and any changes in laws or regulations can impact their structure, issuance, and returns. For example, regulations that affect the **risk retention rules** (requiring

CLO managers to retain a portion of the CLO's equity tranche) could affect the manager's incentive to properly monitor and manage the loan pool. Regulatory changes could also affect the **capital treatment** of CLOs for financial institutions or change tax treatment, affecting investor returns.

- **Basel III and Risk Retention**: Under **Basel III** regulations, banks and other financial institutions are required to hold higher levels of capital against certain structured products, including CLOs. These regulations also include **risk retention requirements**, meaning CLO managers must retain at least 5% of the equity tranche to align their interests with investors. Changes in these requirements or the interpretation of these rules could affect the pricing or attractiveness of CLOs, especially for institutional investors.
- **Dodd-Frank Act**: In the U.S., the **Dodd-Frank Act** includes provisions that affect structured products like CLOs. Specifically, the act imposes certain disclosure, transparency, and risk retention rules. Any potential revisions to Dodd-Frank could impact the CLO market, introducing new compliance risks.
- **Tax Risks**: CLOs have tax-advantaged structures in some jurisdictions, but tax laws can change over time. Regulatory or tax law changes affecting the structure of CLOs (such as shifting from pass-through treatment to regular corporate tax treatment) could introduce risks to the income distributions to CLO investors.

3. Legal Disputes and Litigation

- **Legal Disputes with Borrowers**: CLOs may face legal risks if disputes arise with borrowers over the terms of the loans or in cases of default. For instance, disagreements over loan workouts or the interpretation of loan covenants may lead to litigation, which can delay the resolution of defaults or result in lower recoveries.

- **CLO Manager Disputes**: The CLO manager is responsible for managing the loan pool, but in cases of underperformance or mismanagement, investors may seek legal action against the manager. If a CLO manager fails to follow the proper legal or fiduciary duties, it could lead to legal disputes over losses incurred or mismanagement of the loan pool.
- **Investor Class Action**: If a CLO underperforms or a default event occurs, investors in different tranches may seek legal recourse through class action lawsuits or individual litigation. These legal disputes can further complicate the CLO's performance and delay payouts to investors.
- **Bankruptcy and Insolvency**: If a CLO issuer faces bankruptcy or is involved in an insolvency proceeding, legal complications can arise related to the distribution of the underlying loans, as well as the rights of senior versus junior tranche holders. Bankruptcy proceedings can also delay repayment to investors and lower the recovery rate on CLO investments.

4. Structural and Documentation Risks

- **Complex Legal Documentation**: CLOs are highly structured products, and the legal documentation governing these transactions can be intricate. Investors must fully understand the terms and conditions in CLO documents (such as the indenture or loan agreements) to assess risks properly. Errors in documentation or ambiguous terms can lead to disputes between investors, CLO managers, or borrowers, particularly regarding priority of claims or payment waterfalls.

- **CLO Manager Actions**: CLO managers have significant discretion in managing the portfolio of loans. If the CLO manager takes actions that breach the legal terms outlined in the CLO documents (e.g., investing in higher-risk loans without proper disclosure or approval), legal challenges can arise from investors, especially those in senior tranches.
- **Payment Waterfall Disputes**: The payment waterfall determines how cash flows from the CLO's underlying loans are allocated among different tranches. Disagreements can arise about how cash flows are distributed or about whether the CLO manager adhered to the terms of the CLO agreement, leading to legal risks.

5. Legal Risks Relating to CLO Tranche Ratings

- **Rating Agency Risk**: CLOs rely heavily on credit ratings from rating agencies (e.g., Moody's, S&P, Fitch). If a rating agency downgrades the CLO or specific tranches, it can lead to disputes regarding the interpretation of the rating and whether the CLO is still performing as expected. Rating downgrades could also trigger certain provisions in CLO documentation, like triggering collateral or other financial tests, which could lead to legal ramifications.
- **Due Diligence and Disclosures**: CLO managers are required to conduct due diligence on the loans they include in the CLO pool. If there is inadequate due diligence or failure to disclose material information, investors may have grounds for legal action if the CLO underperforms or defaults due to risks that were not properly identified or disclosed.

6. Cross-Border Legal Risks

- **Jurisdictional Issues**: CLOs may invest in loans issued by companies in multiple jurisdictions. This exposes CLO investors to the risk of differing legal frameworks, where legal protections, bankruptcy laws, and recovery processes may vary across countries. Cross-border legal issues could complicate loan workouts, restructuring efforts, or debt recovery processes.
- **Enforcement of Loan Agreements**: If a borrower is based in a different jurisdiction, enforcing loan agreements, especially in cases of default, can become more complex. Different legal standards or differences in how insolvency and bankruptcy proceedings are handled across borders could lead to delays in repayment or reduced recovery rates for CLO investors.

7. Reputation Risk

- **Reputation of CLO Managers and Servicers**: CLO investors are also exposed to reputation risk. If a CLO manager or servicer becomes involved in a legal dispute or controversy, the reputation of the CLO itself could be damaged. This can impact investor confidence and lead to increased regulatory scrutiny or a reduction in the CLO's value.

Mitigating Legal Risks:

To mitigate legal risks, CLO investors should:

- **Conduct Thorough Due Diligence**: Assess the CLO manager's track record, legal documentation, and underlying assets.
- **Monitor Regulatory Changes**: Stay informed about regulatory changes, particularly around risk retention, tax

laws, and disclosure requirements.
- **Legal Counsel**: Engage legal counsel to evaluate CLO documentation and ensure compliance with regulations.
- **Diversify Investments**: Spread investments across various tranches or CLOs to reduce exposure to specific legal risks related to individual loans or CLO managers.

Investing in CLOs involves navigating a complex legal landscape, including credit risk, regulatory challenges, structural complexities, and potential litigation. Legal risks can significantly impact CLO performance, making it essential for investors to understand the legal framework governing CLOs and to actively manage and mitigate these risks. Legal due diligence, understanding CLO documentation, and staying informed about regulatory changes are all crucial to successful CLO investment strategies.

Here are a few charts that visually represent some of the key concepts around **Collateralized Loan Obligation (CLO) Legal Risks**:

1. Breakdown of CLO Legal Risks

This chart categorizes the various legal risks involved in CLO investments:

Legal Risk Category	Description
Credit & Default Risk	Risk of borrower defaults, affecting CLO performance and recoveries.
Regulatory & Compliance Risk	Changes in regulations, such as Basel III or Dodd-Frank, impacting CLO structures.
Litigation & Disputes	Legal disputes arising from loan defaults, CLO manager actions, or tranche disagreements.
Structural &	Legal risks due to the complexity of

Legal Risk Category	Description
Documentation Risk	CLO structures, documentation, and misinterpretation.
CLO Rating Risks	Risk from downgrades in CLO ratings, leading to changes in investor returns.
Cross-Border Legal Risks	Legal complications in jurisdictions with differing bankruptcy and enforcement laws.

2. CLO Tranche Legal Risk Distribution

This chart visualizes the exposure to legal risks by CLO tranche type. **Equity tranches** carry the highest risk, followed by **mezzanine** and **senior tranches**.

CLO Tranche	Legal Risk Exposure	Risk Level
Equity Tranches	Highest Risk (due to default risk and legal disputes over cash flow allocation)	High
Mezzanine Tranches (BB, B)	Moderate Risk (exposure to defaults and legal disputes)	Medium
Senior Tranches (AAA, AA, A)	Lowest Risk (priority of payment and legal protections)	Low

3. Regulatory Impact on CLO Risk (Example of Regulatory Changes)

This chart demonstrates the potential impact of regulatory changes, such as **Basel III** or **Dodd-Frank**, on CLO risk exposure over time.

Regulatory Event	Potential Impact on CLOs	Effect on Legal Risks
Basel III Implementation	Higher capital requirements for	Increases compliance risk and cost

Regulatory Event	Potential Impact on CLOs	Effect on Legal Risks
	CLOs from financial institutions	
Risk Retention Rules (Dodd-Frank)	CLO managers must retain 5% of CLO equity	Reduces agency risk but increases CLO manager responsibility
Changes to Risk Retention Rules	Potential reduction in risk retention requirements	Potentially increases risk for investors due to weaker alignment of interests

4. CLO Loan Default Risk

This chart shows the effect of loan defaults within a CLO pool. The **percentage of loans defaulting** directly impacts the **recovery rate** and **overall performance** of the CLO.

Default Rate (%)	Recovery Rate	Risk to CLO Investors
0-5% Default	**80-100%**	Low Risk
5-10% Default	**60-80%**	Medium Risk
10-20% Default	**40-60%**	High Risk
>20% Default	**<40%**	Very High Risk

5. CLO Legal Risk Distribution by Region (Cross-Border Risks)

This chart illustrates how legal risks may vary by region due to differences in bankruptcy laws, enforcement, and jurisdictional complexities.

Region	Legal Risk Type	Risk Level
North	Strong legal frameworks for CLOs and	Medium

Region	Legal Risk Type	Risk Level
America	loan enforcement	
Europe	Legal complexity in multiple jurisdictions (e.g., EU, UK, non-EU countries)	High
Emerging Markets	Greater risk from weaker legal systems and enforcement issues	Very High

These charts help visualize the various legal risks associated with CLO investments and how they might impact investors, managers, and the CLO structure itself.

Below are diagrams that visually represent the key concepts around **Collateralized Loan Obligation (CLO) Legal Risks**. These diagrams help to simplify the understanding of CLO structures, legal risks, and their distribution across various components.

1. CLO Structure and Risk Distribution

This diagram represents how legal risks are distributed across different **CLO tranches** based on their seniority.

```
                CLO Structure and Risk Distribution
                    +----------------------------+
                    |        CLO Pool of          |
                    |    Leveraged Loans          |
                    +----------------------------+
                                |
   +------------------------
+------------------------+
   |                            |
|
   |                    Senior Tranches
Mezzanine Tranches
   |                        (Low Risk)
(Moderate Risk)
   |        +-------------------------+
+--------------------+
   |        |  AAA, AA, A, BBB Tranches|        |
BB, B Tranches |
   |        |   - Credit Risk Low      |        |
- Default Risk     |
   |        |   - Priority of Payment  |        |
- Payment Risks    |
   |        +-------------------------+
+--------------------+
   |
   +----------------------------+
   |         Equity Tranches      |
   |         (High Risk)          |
   |    - Exposure to Defaults    |
   |    - First Losses            |
   |    - Legal Disputes in      |
   |      Payment Waterfall      |
   +----------------------------+
```

Explanation:

- **Senior tranches (AAA, AA, A)** face the **lowest legal risk**, as they are paid first and have more legal protections.
- **Mezzanine tranches (BB, B)** come with a **moderate level**

of legal risk, particularly due to potential loan defaults or disputes over the loan management.

- **Equity tranches** carry the **highest legal risk**, as they are the first to experience losses and face complex legal battles during defaults or restructuring processes.

2. Legal Risk Distribution in CLOs

This diagram shows how legal risks vary across different CLO structures, including **credit risk**, **regulatory risk**, and **litigation risk**.

```
                    Legal Risk Distribution in
CLOs
                                  |

+-----------------------------------------+
         |

|
     +---+---+
+---+---+
     | Credit |
| Regulatory |
     | Risk   |
| Risk       |
     | (Defaults and Recovery)
| (Rule Changes, Capital Requirements) |
     +---+---+
+---+---+
         |

|
     +----+----+
+----+----+
     | Litigation|
| Structural|
     | Risk        |
| & Documentation |
     | (Legal Disputes, Tranche Payment
```

```
Issues)        | (CLO Manager, Legal Terms)
|
       +-----------+
+-------------------+
```

Explanation:

- **Credit risk** involves loan defaults, and legal risks around loan recovery.
- **Regulatory risk** refers to potential changes in laws and rules that govern CLOs, such as Basel III or Dodd-Frank regulations.
- **Litigation risk** arises from potential disputes between investors, CLO managers, and borrowers.
- **Structural & Documentation risk** relates to issues arising from complex legal agreements and CLO documentation misinterpretation.

3. CLO Default and Recovery Diagram

This diagram illustrates how **loan defaults** within a CLO pool impact the **recovery rate** for different CLO tranches.

```
                       CLO Default and Recovery Impact

+---------------------------+
                        |      CLO Loan Pool
|
                        |     (Leveraged Loans)
|

+---------------------------+
                                              |
              +-------------------
+--------------------+
              |
|
      +-------+-------+
```

```
+-----+-----+
      | Default Rate  |                          |
Recovery  |
      | (Percentage)   |                          |
Rate        |
      | 0-5%           |                          |
80-100%   |
      | (Low Risk)     |                          |
(Low Risk)|
      +-------+-------+
+-----+-----+
               |
|
    +---------+----------+
+-----------+----------+
    |  Default Rate:      |              | Default
Rate:              |
    |   5-10%             |              | 10-20%
|
    |   (Moderate Risk)   |              | (High
Risk)                 |
    +---------+----------+
+-----------+----------+
               |
|
         +-----+-------+
+----+-------+
         | Recovery Rate:|
| Recovery Rate: |
         | 60-80%        |
| 40-60%         |
         | (Medium Risk) |
| (High Risk)    |
```

Explanation:

- If the **default rate** is low (0-5%), the **recovery rate** for investors is high (80-100%) with **low legal risk**.
- If the **default rate** increases (5-10%), the **recovery rate** decreases to 60-80%, raising the legal and recovery risks for investors.
- At high default levels (>10%), **recovery rates** drop significantly (40-60%), leading to **high legal risks** and significant investor losses.

4. Regulatory Impact on CLOs

This diagram shows how **regulatory changes** (such as **Basel III** or **Dodd-Frank**) can affect CLO structures and **legal risks** over time.

```
                          Regulatory Impact on CLOs
                                  |

+-------------------------------------------------+
      |
|
  +----+-----+
+-----+----+
  | Basel III |
| Dodd-Frank |
  | Regulation |
| Act          |
  | (Capital    |
| (Risk Retention)|
  | Requirements)|
| (Disclosure Rules)|
  +-----------+
+-------------+
      |
|
+------v-------+
+----v----+
```

```
| Compliance   |
| Risk     |
| Costs        |
| Retention |
| (Higher Capital)|
| (Manager Retains 5%)|
+--------------+
+------------+
```

Explanation:

- **Basel III** regulations increase the **capital requirements** for financial institutions investing in CLOs, adding **compliance costs** and affecting CLO issuance.
- **Dodd-Frank** introduces **risk retention rules** requiring CLO managers to retain 5% of the CLO equity tranche, increasing the manager's responsibility and aligning interests with investors.

These diagrams provide a simplified visual representation of the **legal risks** associated with CLO investments, helping investors better understand the structure, regulatory influences, and potential legal issues that may arise during the lifecycle of a CLO.

COLLATERALIZED
LOAN OBLIGATION

CHAPTER 12:HOW TO MAKE MONEY USING COLLATERALIZED LOAN OBLIGATIONS

Collateralized Loan Obligations (CLOs) can be a lucrative investment strategy if approached carefully. CLOs are structured financial products that pool together loans, typically leveraged loans, and divide them into tranches (layers) with varying levels of risk and return. The way to make money with CLOs depends on your position in the CLO structure, how you manage risks, and market conditions. Here's how investors can profit from CLOs:

1. Investing in Senior CLO Tranches (Low Risk, Stable Returns)

Senior tranches in a CLO are the highest-rated and generally provide the most stable returns. These tranches are the first to be paid out in the event of loan payments, which reduces their exposure to defaults.

- *How to Make Money*:
    - **Coupon Payments**: Senior CLO tranches typically pay regular coupon payments, which are determined by the interest rates on the underlying loans. Investors in senior tranches typically earn a steady income stream from these payments.
    - **Less Risk of Loss**: Since senior tranches are paid first, they are the least exposed to defaults and losses. This means they offer more predictable and safer returns compared to lower-rated tranches.
    - **Potential Return**: The yields on senior CLO tranches are typically **3-6%**, depending on the quality of the underlying loans and the interest rate environment.
- **Example**:

- You invest in a **AAA-rated senior tranche** of a CLO, and the underlying leveraged loans have an average interest rate of 5%. You might earn an annual coupon payment of 5% on your investment, with relatively lower risk of losing principal.

2. Investing in Mezzanine or Subordinated CLO Tranches (Higher Risk, Higher Return)

Mezzanine and subordinated tranches (including BB and B-rated tranches) carry more risk but also offer higher returns. These tranches are lower in the CLO structure, meaning they are paid after the senior tranches, making them more vulnerable to defaults in the loan pool.

- ***How to Make Money***:
  - **Higher Yields**: Investors in mezzanine and subordinated tranches receive higher yields (often in the range of **6-12%** or more), which compensate for the additional risk they take on by being lower in the payment hierarchy.
  - **Credit Risk**: While these tranches offer higher returns, the risk of losing money is greater. If the underlying loans in the CLO pool experience defaults, the investors in the mezzanine or subordinated tranches are more likely to bear the brunt of the losses.
  - **Potential Upside**: In the case of a strong-performing loan pool with few defaults, mezzanine and subordinated tranche investors can realize substantial gains due to the higher yields and a larger portion of the CLO's cash flows once the senior tranches are paid off.
- **Example**:
  - You invest in a **B-rated mezzanine tranche**, which

has a yield of 10%. If the CLO's underlying loans perform well and there are few defaults, you could earn 10% annually, with higher returns than senior tranches but also with higher exposure to potential losses.

3. Trading CLOs in the Secondary Market (Capital Gains)

CLOs are traded in the secondary market, and investors can make money by buying CLO securities at a discount and selling them at a premium, or by holding them to maturity.

- **How to Make Money**:
  - **Capital Gains**: If market conditions are favorable (e.g., interest rates fall or the economy improves), the value of CLO securities can increase. Buying CLO tranches when they are undervalued and selling them when their market price appreciates can lead to capital gains.
  - **Price Movements**: CLO tranches, especially those with lower ratings, can be volatile. If the market perceives that the underlying loans are performing better than expected (e.g., fewer defaults), the prices of CLO tranches may rise, allowing investors to sell for a profit.
  - **Interest Rate Sensitivity**: CLOs are also sensitive to interest rate changes. If interest rates rise, floating-rate loans in the CLO pool will generate higher income, which could increase the value of CLO securities. Conversely, if rates fall, the CLO's yield could decrease, causing prices to fall.
- **Example**:
  - You buy a **BB-rated tranche** of a CLO when it is undervalued due to short-term market concerns. Over time, the market stabilizes, defaults decrease,

and the CLO's cash flow improves, driving up the price. You sell the CLO at a higher price, realizing a capital gain.

4. Structuring and Managing CLOs (CLO Manager Fees)

CLO managers are responsible for the day-to-day operation of a CLO, including selecting and managing the loans that back the CLO, handling the payments to investors, and managing the risks within the CLO portfolio. CLO managers typically earn fees based on the size of the CLO and its performance.

- **How to Make Money**:
    - **Management Fees**: CLO managers earn **management fees** for overseeing the CLO's operations. These fees are typically a percentage of the CLO's total assets or equity.
    - **Incentive Fees**: CLO managers can also earn **incentive fees** if the CLO generates returns above a certain threshold. This incentivizes the manager to actively manage the CLO to optimize returns for investors.
    - **Fee Structure**: Typically, the fee structure involves a base management fee (usually around **0.5-1%** of the total assets) and a performance-based incentive fee (ranging from **10-20%** of profits over a specific hurdle rate).
- **Example**:
    - A CLO manager might earn an **annual management fee** of 1% of the total value of a CLO, along with an **incentive fee** if the CLO outperforms a specified return threshold.

5. CLO Investment Funds (Indirect Exposure)

For individual investors who do not want to directly buy CLO securities, there are **CLO investment funds** or **CLO ETFs** that allow for indirect exposure to CLOs. These funds pool capital from multiple investors to purchase CLO securities.

- **How to Make Money**:
    - **Dividend Income**: CLO funds or ETFs distribute income generated from the interest payments of the underlying CLO loans. Depending on the fund's focus (e.g., senior vs. mezzanine CLOs), investors can earn **regular dividends** or income from CLO returns.
    - **Diversification**: By investing in CLO funds or ETFs, investors gain diversified exposure to a broad portfolio of CLO tranches, which helps reduce the risks associated with any single CLO.
- **Example**:
    - You invest in a **CLO ETF** such as the **Invesco Senior Loan ETF (BKLN)**, which tracks a portfolio of senior loans and CLOs. The ETF pays out regular dividends based on the income generated from the underlying CLOs.

6. Hedging with CLOs

Some sophisticated investors use CLOs as a **hedging tool** to manage interest rate or credit risk. CLOs can be used in a broader portfolio of fixed-income securities to balance the exposure to rising interest rates or defaults.

- **How to Make Money**:
    - **Risk Mitigation**: CLOs can help hedge against specific risks in a broader portfolio. For example, investors with heavy exposure to interest rate-

sensitive assets (e.g., long-duration bonds) might buy CLOs, which have floating rates and tend to perform better in rising interest rate environments.

- **Example**:
    - If you have a portfolio of long-term government bonds that are vulnerable to rising interest rates, you might add CLOs to your portfolio. CLOs' floating-rate nature could offset the impact of rising rates on other parts of your portfolio.

Making money with **Collateralized Loan Obligations (CLOs)** can take many forms depending on your investment strategy, risk appetite, and market conditions. Whether you are seeking **steady income** from senior tranches, **high returns** from mezzanine tranches, **capital gains** from trading CLOs, or **managerial fees** from managing CLO portfolios, there are several ways to profit from CLOs. However, it is crucial to understand the **risks** involved, such as **credit risk**, **interest rate risk**, and **liquidity risk**, to make informed investment decisions.

Who Buys Collateralized Loan Obligations (CLOs)?

Collateralized Loan Obligations (CLOs) are purchased by a variety of institutional investors, each with specific investment strategies, risk profiles, and objectives. The buyers of CLOs include entities that are looking for exposure to leveraged loans, typically high-yield debt, with the potential for higher returns. These investors often seek a mix of income and diversification while balancing the associated risks. Below are the key types of investors who buy CLOs:

1. Institutional Investors

a) Insurance Companies

- **Why They Buy CLOs**: Insurance companies, particularly **life insurers**, are significant buyers of CLOs because they are looking for stable, long-term income streams to match their liabilities, such as policyholder claims. CLOs, especially **senior tranches**, provide **steady yields** that are attractive compared to traditional fixed-income products.

- **Risk Profile**: They typically invest in higher-rated CLO tranches (e.g., **AAA, AA, A**) to minimize risk.

b) Pension Funds

- **Why They Buy CLOs**: Pension funds seek to meet long-term liabilities with a diversified portfolio. CLOs provide **higher yields** than traditional government bonds or investment-grade corporate bonds, helping pension funds achieve their required return targets.
- **Risk Profile**: Pension funds generally focus on **senior tranches** or **investment-grade** CLO tranches to reduce exposure to credit risk.

c) Hedge Funds

- **Why They Buy CLOs**: Hedge funds often seek higher returns and are willing to take on **greater risk** in exchange for higher yield. Some hedge funds specialize in CLOs, using them to gain exposure to **leveraged loans** or by purchasing specific CLO tranches with attractive risk-return profiles.
- **Risk Profile**: Hedge funds are typically more flexible in investing in **higher-risk tranches**, including mezzanine (e.g., **BB**, **B**) and equity tranches, in order to capture **potentially higher returns**.

d) Asset Managers and Investment Firms

- **Why They Buy CLOs**: Asset managers, including mutual funds and other managed funds, invest in CLOs to provide clients with exposure to diversified **loan portfolios** that yield higher returns than traditional fixed-income investments.
- **Risk Profile**: These investors can invest across all CLO tranches, though they tend to focus on **senior** or **mezzanine tranches**, depending on the fund's risk tolerance.

2. Commercial Banks

- **Why They Buy CLOs**: Commercial banks may invest in CLOs as part of their broader investment strategy to earn higher yields from

loan portfolios while maintaining diversified risk. Banks may also purchase CLOs to hold as assets on their balance sheets, particularly when they need exposure to senior tranches for regulatory or strategic reasons.
- **Risk Profile**: Banks tend to favor **senior CLO tranches** because of their lower credit risk.

3. Private Equity Firms

- **Why They Buy CLOs**: Private equity firms sometimes purchase CLOs as part of their broader strategy to gain access to leveraged loans or to restructure CLOs to generate additional returns for their investors.
- **Risk Profile**: Private equity firms may invest in **mezzanine tranches** or even **equity tranches** of CLOs to capitalize on the **higher potential returns**. However, this exposes them to greater risk, as these tranches are the first to absorb losses in case of defaults.

4. Sovereign Wealth Funds

- **Why They Buy CLOs**: Sovereign wealth funds (SWFs) may invest in CLOs as part of their diversified portfolio strategy, seeking exposure to alternative assets with high yield potential. CLOs fit well into a long-term investment strategy for SWFs, especially those with mandates to earn higher returns while managing risk.
- **Risk Profile**: SWFs tend to focus on more stable, high-grade CLO tranches (e.g., **AAA** or **AA**) but may also take some exposure to lower-rated tranches for enhanced yield.

5. Family Offices

- **Why They Buy CLOs**: Family offices often manage the wealth of high-net-worth individuals or families and seek investments that provide **higher yields** and **portfolio diversification**. CLOs can be an attractive investment for those looking to balance income and risk.
- **Risk Profile**: Depending on the family office's risk appetite, it may invest in a wide range of CLO tranches, but many family offices prefer **senior** or **mezzanine tranches** for more stable returns.

6. Exchange-Traded Funds (ETFs) and Closed-End Funds (CEFs)

- **Why They Buy CLOs**: ETFs and CEFs focused on CLOs offer retail and institutional investors a convenient way to gain exposure to CLO markets without directly purchasing individual CLO securities. These funds typically pool investments from various investors and buy CLO tranches as part of a diversified portfolio.
- **Risk Profile**: These funds may invest across a range of CLO tranches, including **senior**, **mezzanine**, and **equity tranches**, depending on their strategy. However, CLO ETFs and CEFs usually focus on **more diversified** tranches, typically avoiding high-risk equity tranches.

7. CLO Managers (Issuers of CLOs)

- **Why They Buy CLOs**: In some cases, CLO managers (the firms that create and manage CLOs) may hold CLO securities on their own balance sheets. These managers might retain some tranches for their own portfolios as part of their **alignment of interests** with investors, particularly the **equity tranches**.
- **Risk Profile**: CLO managers often buy **equity tranches** because of the potential for high returns, but these are also the riskiest tranches in the CLO structure.

8. Retail Investors (Indirect Exposure via Funds)

- **Why They Buy CLOs**: Retail investors typically gain exposure to CLOs indirectly through **CLO mutual funds**, **ETFs**, or **CLO-focused funds**. These funds provide diversified exposure to a range of CLO tranches and enable retail investors to invest in the CLO market without directly purchasing individual CLO securities.
- **Risk Profile**: Retail investors typically invest in CLO funds that focus on **senior tranches** or more conservative **mezzanine tranches**, which tend to offer lower risk compared to the equity tranches.

Summary of Who Buys CLOs and Why:

Investor Type	Reason for Buying CLOs	Typical Risk Profile
Insurance Companies	Stable, long-term income streams to match liabilities	Senior tranches (Low risk, Stable returns)
Pension Funds	Diversification and higher yield for long-term liabilities	Senior or Investment-Grade Tranches (Low risk)
Hedge Funds	Seeking high returns and willing to take on more risk	Mezzanine and Equity Tranches (Higher risk, High returns)
Asset Managers	Diversification, income generation, and portfolio growth	Senior or Mezzanine Tranches (Medium risk)
Commercial Banks	Investment and regulatory needs	Senior Tranches (Low risk)
Private Equity Firms	Access to leveraged loans or CLO restructuring	Mezzanine and Equity Tranches (High risk)
Sovereign Wealth Funds	Long-term growth and portfolio diversification	Senior Tranches (Low risk)
Family Offices	Diversification, wealth preservation, and growth	Senior or Mezzanine Tranches (Medium risk)
ETFs and CEFs	Offer CLO exposure to retail and institutional investors	Varies by fund strategy (Risk levels depend on focus)
CLO Managers	Alignment of interest with investors, high returns	Equity Tranches (High risk)

In essence, **institutional investors** dominate the CLO market, but there is a growing presence of **retail investors** through **funds**. CLOs offer diverse ways to generate returns, from stable income to higher-yield, riskier options, attracting a broad range of buyers with varying risk appetites.

FAQ

What is the difference between a CDO and a CLO? What is CLO and how does it work? How does a CLO manager make money? What is the difference between a CLO and a bdc?

1. What is the difference between a CDO and a CLO?

Collateralized Debt Obligation (CDO) and **Collateralized Loan Obligation (CLO)** are both types of asset-backed securities (ABS), but there are significant differences between them:

- **Underlying Assets**:
    - A **CDO** is typically backed by a variety of debt instruments, such as mortgage-backed securities (MBS), corporate bonds, and other types of debt.
    - A **CLO** is specifically backed by a pool of loans made to corporations, usually non-investment grade loans or leveraged loans, which are often made to companies with higher risk profiles.
- **Risk Profile**:
    - **CDOs** can include a wider range of asset classes, so their risk profile can be more diversified but also more complex. CDOs can also be more exposed to the housing market if they include mortgage-backed securities.
    - **CLOs**, being backed specifically by corporate loans, are more focused on the credit risk of corporations and are often seen as less susceptible to volatility in other markets like real estate.
- **Investor Focus**:
    - **CDOs** often appeal to investors who are looking for exposure to different debt instruments, including mortgage-backed securities and corporate bonds.
    - **CLOs** tend to appeal more to investors focused on the corporate debt market, especially those looking for high-yield (riskier) loans.

2. What is a CLO and how does it work?

A **Collateralized Loan Obligation (CLO)** is a financial product that pools together loans made to corporations, particularly non-investment grade companies (high-yield or leveraged loans), and then divides this pool into different tranches. Each tranche represents a different level of risk and return.

Here's how it works:

- **Loan Pool**: A CLO is backed by a pool of corporate loans, which can include loans from various companies, usually with varying degrees of credit risk. These loans are typically non-investment grade, meaning they are higher risk but also offer the potential for higher returns.
- **Tranches**: The CLO is divided into several tranches, each with a different level of risk and return. The tranches are ranked by seniority, with the highest-ranked (senior) tranches receiving payments first, while the lower-ranked (equity) tranches receive payments last but have the potential for higher returns.
- **CLO Manager**: A CLO manager actively manages the pool of loans, buying and selling loans within the pool to optimize returns and manage risk. The manager may reinvest proceeds from the loans to improve the CLO's performance.
- **Payments**: Investors in the CLO receive payments based on the tranche they invest in. Senior tranches are paid first and typically offer lower yields, while junior tranches (including equity tranches) are paid last and offer higher yields.

3. How does a CLO manager make money?

A **CLO manager** makes money by actively managing the pool of loans that back the CLO. The primary ways they generate income are:

- **Management Fees**: CLO managers typically charge an annual management fee, which is a percentage of the assets under management (AUM) of the CLO. This fee is typically a small percentage of the CLO's total value.

- **Incentive Fees**: In addition to management fees, CLO managers can earn **incentive fees**, which are based on the CLO's performance. If the CLO generates returns above a certain threshold (called a "hurdle rate"), the manager is entitled to a portion of the profits. This aligns the interests of the CLO manager with the investors, as the manager has an incentive to generate strong returns.

- **Reinvestment**: CLO managers can also make money by reinvesting the proceeds from loan repayments or by selling loans that are performing well. If they manage to buy loans at a discount or sell them for a premium, they can increase the CLO’s value, benefiting both themselves and the CLO's investors.

4. What is the difference between a CLO and a BDC?

A **Business Development Company (BDC)** and a **Collateralized Loan Obligation (CLO)** are both investment vehicles that deal with corporate loans, but they have different structures and purposes.

- **Structure**:
  - A **BDC** is a company that invests in small or mid-sized businesses, typically in the form of loans or equity investments. BDCs are publicly traded on stock exchanges and are required by law to distribute at least 90% of their taxable income to shareholders in the form of dividends.
  - A **CLO**, on the other hand, is a special-purpose vehicle (SPV) that pools loans made to various companies and divides these loans into different tranches that are sold to investors.
- **Investment Strategy**:
  - **BDCs** primarily focus on investing in private companies, often providing capital to companies that are not able to access traditional financing sources. BDCs may also provide both debt and equity financing to these companies.
  - **CLOs** focus solely on pools of corporate loans, primarily leveraged loans, from a diverse range of companies. CLOs are generally more structured in terms of risk-sharing among investors through the use of tranches.
- **Investor Returns**:
  - **BDCs** typically generate income for investors through dividends, as they are required to distribute a large portion of their income. They also offer potential capital gains from equity investments in businesses.

    - **CLOs** generate returns through the payments made on the loans in the pool, with investors in senior tranches receiving more consistent but lower yields, and investors in equity tranches receiving higher returns but with more risk.
- **Regulatory Differences**:
    - **BDCs** are regulated under the Investment Company Act of 1940, and they must meet certain requirements, such as offering liquidity and providing investors with regular income through dividends.
    - **CLOs** are not regulated in the same way and are more complex, structured investment vehicles. They are governed by securities laws but do not have the same regulatory requirements as BDCs.

In summary:

- A **BDC** is a public company that invests in smaller, private businesses and distributes its income to investors, while a **CLO** is a structured security backed by corporate loans, offering different tranches with varying levels of risk and return.

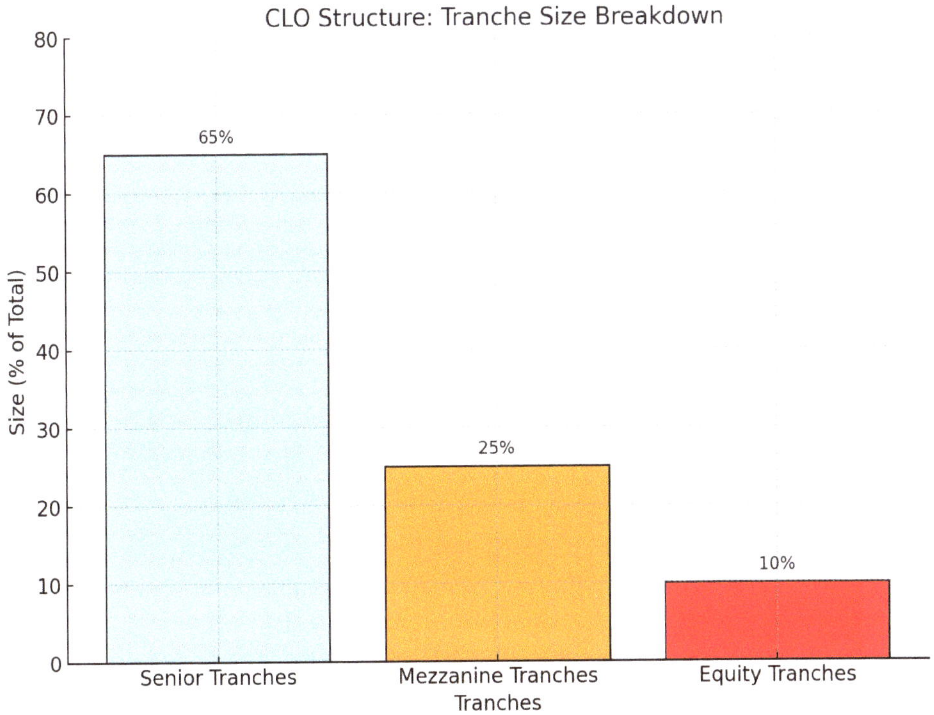

Here's a bar chart displaying the approximate size breakdown of Collateralized Loan Obligation (CLO) tranches. The chart highlights the proportions of Senior, Mezzanine, and Equity tranches in a typical CLO structure. Let me know if you'd like to add more details or comparisons!

Conclusion

Collateralized Loan Obligations (CLOs) are sophisticated financial instruments designed to provide investment opportunities across a range of risk and return profiles. Their structured hierarchy, consisting of senior, mezzanine, and equity tranches, allows investors to select positions based on their risk tolerance and desired yield.

The **senior tranches** offer stability and low default risk, making them suitable for conservative investors, while the **mezzanine tranches** strike a balance between moderate risk and return. For those willing to take on significant risk for potentially higher returns, the **equity tranches** provide a compelling option, albeit with no guarantees of repayment.

CLOs are actively managed, ensuring the portfolio remains balanced and credit quality is preserved. With mechanisms like over-collateralization and diversification, CLOs mitigate some of the inherent risks associated with leveraged loans. Their lifecycle—from ramp-up to maturity—ensures an organized process for generating and distributing cash flows.

Ultimately, CLOs play a vital role in the financial ecosystem by providing liquidity to corporate borrowers and attractive investment opportunities for diverse investor classes. However, their complexity requires a solid understanding of their structure and associated risks before investing.

Table of Contents

www.ingramcontent.com/pod-product-compliance
Lightning Source LLC
LaVergne TN
LVHW051103210926
848486LV00019B/406